Once Upon a Pesto:
Master the Pesto Process with 120 Internationally-Inspired Recipes

© 2025 Jessica Paholsky
All Rights Reserved

Cover Design and Interior Composition by Rachel Loughlin
rachelloughlin.com

Published by Library Tales Publishing
WWW.LIBRARYTALESPUBLISHING.COM

No part of this publication may be reproduced, stored in a retrieval system, or transmitted in any form or by any means, electronic, mechanical, photocopying, recording, scanning, or otherwise, except as permitted under Sections 107 or 108 of the 1976 United States Copyright Act, without the prior written permission of the Publisher. Requests to the Publisher for permission should be addressed to the Legal Department: Legal@LibraryTales.com

Trademarks: Library Tales Publishing, Library Tales, the Library Tales Publishing logo, and related trade dress are trademarks or registered trademarks of Library Tales Publishing and/or its affiliates in the United States and other countries, and may not be used without written permission. All other trademarks are the property of their respective owners.

Printed and published in the United States of America

9798894410227

Once Upon A Pesto

MASTER THE PESTO PROCESS WITH
120 INTERNATIONALLY-INSPIRED RECIPES

JESSICA PAHOLSKY

Table Of Contents

About the Author — 5

Forward — 6

History and Introduction: Mastering the Pesto Process — 8

How To Use This Book — 10

Part 1 (Chapters 1-10): The Americas — 14
The first ten chapters of Once Upon a Pesto explore the cultures and countries that comprise historic and modern-day North, Central, and South America: Native American, Mayan, Southern United States, the Midwest United States, New York, Canada, Puerto Rico, Peru, Chile, and Brazil.

Part 2 (Chapters 11-20): Europe — 76
The next ten chapters of Once Upon a Pesto explore ten European nations: Spain, France, Belgium, Sweden, Switzerland, Italy, Croatia, Greece, Cyprus, and Georgia.

Part 3 (Chapters 21-30): Asia — 138
The third "part" of Once Upon a Pesto covers ten unique culinary gems in Asia: Armenia, Iran, India, Russia, China, Korea, Japan, Malaysia, Thailand, and Myanmar.

Part 4 (Chapters 31-40): Africa and Islands — 200
The final ten chapters of Once Upon a Pesto highlight seven countries in Africa as well as three island nations: Morocco, Nigeria, Egypt, Ethiopia, Uganda, Mozambique, South Africa, Australia, New Zealand, and Fiji.

Acknowledgements — 262

Indices — 266

About the Author

JESSICA PAHOLSKY

is the founder, author, recipe developer, and photographer of Once Upon a Pesto. She is a full-time creative communications professional with experience working in the travel, publishing, and education industries. During her undergraduate studies at Penn State University, she was awarded the W. LaMarr Kopp International Achievement Award for her contributions to the advancement of the international mission of the University. Jessica continues to model that vision for global understanding through Once Upon a Pesto. Her story and recipes have been featured in local newspapers, higher education material, regional and global magazines, as well as regional radio, podcast, and television segments.

Forward

Scratch the surface, and you'll walk away with impressions. Dig deeper, and you'll journey into understanding and appreciation. As my college semester abroad in Italy approached, my planning compulsions took hold. I wrote down all the countries I wanted to visit via short flights or train rides during our three-day weekends. However, after the first few days in my new hometown, Perugia, Italy, I canned my plan and committed myself to visiting each of the country's 20 regions over the four-month semester. This grand tour of Italy I mapped for myself proved how much depth there is to a single country. No country, Italy included, can be generalized in any aspect of its being.

Fast forward a few semesters to when I began preparing my Schreyer Honors College thesis proposal. My thesis adviser, Curt Chandler, knew of my passion for Italy and visual storytelling, so he introduced me to a book by Tom Mueller called Extra Virginity: The Sublime and Scandalous World of Olive Oil. Like my four months traveling throughout the Italian peninsula, this book revealed there's often more work required to get the whole story. I returned to Italy on a five-day visit to film the 2013 olive harvest. By winter, I submitted my thesis—a mini-documentary about the truth of extra virgin olive oil, with a written supplement—and graduated from Penn State University with honors in journalism and Italian.

A few days after commencement, I joined Travel For Teens as a full-time staff member and videographer. I spent the next two summers living out of a duffel bag, plus a backpack filled with my camera gear, to document high school students' travel experiences all over the globe. I got to explore for the first time several countries in Europe, China, and Costa Rica. I also adopted the company's motto—"Be a traveler, not a tourist." You could visit all the sites and eat all the best food, but to really understand a country and its culture, you must seek out authentic experiences and look past generalizations.

My college and professional travel experiences paved the way for my mission in Once Upon a Pesto. Having studied Italian for several semesters and building off of my mini-documentary on olive oil, pesto struck me as eclectically mysterious. The more I read, the more I saw similarities of generalization between this sauce and my international awakenings. I was confident there were other people out there who also thought pesto was a specific recipe of basil and pine nuts, served with pasta, and only tied to Italy.

> I wrote this book not only for those other pesto-curious minds, but also for every travel enthusiast, culture discoverer, and foodie— from amateur to pro.

Once Upon a Pesto is a source for practical cooking techniques and recipes as much as it is an indispensable reference for international reading. It's a child-like approach to learn about the foods we eat, the cultures surrounding our very own, and the joy of expanding our minds. I like to think of cooking as a form of art, similar to music or painting. Each can be universally understood despite any language barriers or geographic borders. No matter your age, I hope you are excited to dig deeper with me. You're about to find food and travel as great platforms for learning and living, even from the comfort of your own home.

Jessica Paholsky

History and Introduction:

During the Middle Ages, sauces made with a mortar and pestle helped add flavor to many dishes. The key, and possibly only, ingredient of one 13th-century sauce called aggiadda was garlic. The people of this time believed garlic could ward off illness and evil. Also, due to its association with lower classes, ruling populations hesitated to incorporate garlic into their diets.

Meanwhile, in ancient Rome, another sauce had surfaced. From a Latin word that roughly translates to 'salad,' moretum was a spreadable mixture also made with a mortar and pestle. Sans garlic, it consisted of herbs, fresh cheese, salt, oil, and vinegar. It was typically eaten on bread.

Further north in Italy during the 16th century, these ancient culinary techniques led to the pesto most popular today. In the northwest region called Liguria, specifically in the coastal town of Genoa, basil grew extremely well. The temperate climate paired with the seaside soil were just what this herb needed to thrive.

Basil is not native to Italy, however. It reached Europe via ancient spice routes after its domestication in India. Soon enough, though, Italians claimed basil as their own and saw it as a prime ingredient for sauce. The first recorded recipe for pesto comes from a 19th-century text on Genovese recipes. Pesto Genovese was born.

JESSICA PAHOLSKY

Mastering the Pesto Process

In its name, Genovese acknowledges this sauce's hometown roots in Genoa. The word pesto comes from the Italian verb pestare, which means 'to pound' or 'to crush.' The same verb is what inspired the name pestle. The words pesto and pestle, therefore, signal a process, not a specific set of ingredients. Similar to pesto's ancient predecessors, Italians made pesto Genovese using a mortar and pestle. Even to this day, the tradition of making pesto Genovese by hand is celebrated through experiences and events, such as the biennial Pesto World Championship in Genoa.

In Italy alone, there are several pesto variations. South of Genoa, and even south of Rome, Italians in the region of Calabria looked to their own resources for pesto-making. Their pesto Calabrese features red bell pepper as the key ingredient since that is one of the best local crops. Furthermore, in the Sicilian town of Trapani, tomatoes are the foundation of pesto Trapanese. The common threads among pesto Genovese, pesto Calabrese, and pesto Trapanese are the use of regional produce and a name that identifies the sauces' geographic origins.

With this historic background in mind, pesto offers infinite possibilities, from its ingredients to learning about an area's culture and its people. Without an exact recipe, anyone anywhere can master the pesto process. The ages-old culinary practice is a creative use of local resources and all senses. Pesto-making can also help support local producers, save money through in-season shopping, and enhance flavor among many dishes.

ONCE UPON A PESTO

How To Use This Book

Once Upon a Pesto **is a new way of thinking about how flavors and textures pair with creativity and flexibility on a global scale. Through the pesto-as-a-process approach, you will master pesto-making and discover innovative applications for many pesto recipes.** You can customize pesto to your favorite ingredients and personal food preferences. Whether you have a dairy or nut allergy, you can make pesto to fit your needs. Pesto also allows you to work with regional and seasonal produce based on where you live and what time of year it is; this is great for supporting your local farmers and also for saving some pennies. There are endless possibilities for flavors in pesto, too—from savory to sweet and everything in between.

With this understanding of pesto, you can begin experimenting in your kitchen with different foods and techniques. To make the most of your journey, *Once Upon a Pesto* provides 40 original pesto recipes as well as how to use each in traditional cultural dishes. Every recipe is meant to transport you to a different country or region of the world through flavors and stories.

Rather than dividing the book into courses like breakfasts, main dishes, sides, and desserts, I chose to organize my recipes by geography. The journey is up to you. Take a world tour with recipes from several different countries all in one meal. Or focus on one continent or country at a time.

CONTINENTS

Each of the four parts of this book include ten countries or cultures within a certain continent (or two). You will find wide variations between histories, traditions, and cuisines in each continent represented. The selected countries are meant to represent some of that diversity and also make known ingredients you may not have ventured to try before.

COUNTRIES AND CULTURES

Within each chapter, three recipes paint the picture of a single country or culture. First is an original pesto recipe, which uses one or two key ingredients that are significant to that country or culture. The second and third recipes are two dishes or drinks that incorporate the pesto, and both recipes are in some way important to that country or culture. In addition to the three recipes, each chapter includes supplementary information about the ingredients, dishes, culinary techniques, and history of that country or culture. The goal in each chapter is to provide a better understanding of what it would be like to travel to that part of the world, engage with its people, and experience its traditions.

Now that you know where this book will take you by each section and chapter, it's time to get to the techniques and processes you can use. There are benefits to each approach, so you can choose what's best for you and your situation at any given time.

EQUIPMENT

The tried and true tool for making pesto is the mortar and pestle. A mortar is a bowl where the food is placed, and the pestle is a club-shaped object used to pound the mortar's contents. Dating back to the Stone Age, people use this primitive pair to process ingredients into a mixture. During this process, the individual cells within foods are broken down, and aromas are released. The resulting sauce or blend offers a unique chemistry of flavors and textures. Mortars and pestles come in many different materials,

ONCE UPON A PESTO

from granite or marble to wood or ceramic. No matter the material, using a mortar and pestle to make pesto takes more time and effort; it's human-powered. As a result, it's best for small quantities of pesto. If you are making a larger batch of pesto or want to save time and effort, a food processor or blender are great options. These appliances can turn out a pesto recipe in a matter of seconds. However, the chemical breakdown of ingredients achieved with a mortar and pestle is lacking. Instead, the blades of food processors and blenders chop and whip the ingredients, and all you have to do is push a button. The difference in taste between the same pesto made in a mortar and pestle versus a food processor may be noticeable only to trained palates.

INGREDIENTS

Speaking of palates and taste, every pesto recipe in this book calls for several ingredients. There are one or two main ingredients that are significant to the country or culture of each chapter. The other ingredients add flavor complements, textures, or substance. One of the most magical things about pesto is its customizable essence. The only true required ingredient in pesto is quality food. For example, when making a pesto that calls for olive oil, opt for a good extra virgin olive oil. Similarly, if you have to choose between Parmigiano Reggiano cheese and sprinkled Parmesan cheese, go with the former.

For those with food allergies, sensitivities, or intolerances, one or two ingredients in a single pesto recipe can be modified or omitted without significantly changing the overall nature of the recipe. If nuts or dairy are a concern for you, there are several pesto recipes that fit into the "free" category for each.

JESSICA PAHOLSKY

STORAGE

Once you've made your pesto, you can choose to use it in one or both of the recipes provided for that chapter. If you don't plan to use the pesto right away, you can store it in an airtight container in the refrigerator for up to five or seven days. Or, you can freeze the pesto for up to six months. Upon thawing, note that the liquid texture of the pesto may change based on its ingredients; ingredients with a higher water content are more likely to change in texture upon thawing. Once thawed, the pesto can be used as any given recipe calls for. There are several options for what to store the pesto in, from plastic containers to glass containers or jars. The most important factor to consider when choosing a storage container is that it can be closed airtight.

USE

With any pesto, the opportunities for use are endless. In every chapter of this book, I provide two different recipes in which to use each original pesto recipe. But, you can also incorporate any pesto you make into countless other dishes. Toss the sauce with roasted vegetables. Use it as a dipping sauce for chips or cold vegetables. Or spread it onto a piece of toast or your favorite sandwich. We know from the Ligurian example that pesto pairs great with pasta, but there are so many other avenues to explore this versatile sauce. Start your day with a poached egg drizzled with an herb-based pesto. Stir in a fruit-based pesto with some ricotta cheese, and top that on crackers for a midday snack. Or take your mashed potatoes to a whole new level by mixing in a vegetable-based pesto; it will make your plate more colorful and add a boost of different vitamins. If you can imagine it, it's possible with pesto.

ONCE UPON A PESTO

PART 1: The Americas

One glance at different cuisines around the world, and it's easy to spot American-born foods. From corn and squash to potatoes and chocolate, North and South America have historically paved the way for many culinary staples still thriving today.

It all began with the diverse cultures that first inhabited North America. These various groups of people had their own culinary customs as well as localized food products. In fact, they would travel seasonally to live off of the resources available throughout the land, never settling permanently because that meant insufficient resources during certain times of the year. These hunter-gatherers ate meats such as bison, birds, deer, elk, and some fish like trout. Wild plants in the form of nuts, seeds, wild rice, wild berries, and cacti also provided them sustenance.

Sauce Similarity in the Americas

In South American cuisine, **chimichurri** is a green herb sauce. Specifically, in the countries of Argentina and Uruguay, it's popular both as an ingredient in recipes and as a condiment for topping foods like cooked meat. Contrary to pesto Genovese, *chimichurri's* main ingredient is parsley, not basil, and it also calls for garlic and olive oil.

The origins of this sauce are unclear. Most people would say *gaúchos,* or cowboys, in Argentina developed the sauce to flavor their fire-roasted meats. There is also a tale that claims the name *chimichurri* is a spinoff of the sound of a man's name, Jimmy Curry, who was a European immigrant in the meat-selling industry.

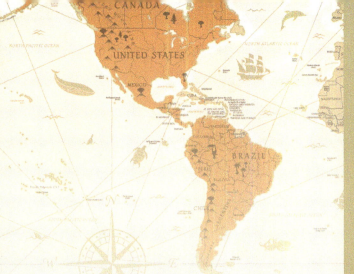

1. NATIVE AMERICAN
2. MAYAN
3. SOUTHERN UNITED STATES
4. THE MIDWEST UNITED STATES
5. NEW YORK
6. CANADA
7. PUERTO RICO
8. PERU
9. CHILE
10. BRAZIL

Eventually, some indigenous populations settled down and formed agriculture-based communities. This led to the domestication of animals for food—one of the first was turkey. They also domesticated some plants, including corn, beans, and squash. These three crops soon became global staples. Now, they form the foundation of many dishes among cultures around the world.

Potatoes also hail from the Americas, specifically South America. Other early harvests from this continent include chili peppers and avocados. These foods were often consumed with minimal processing. On the other hand, maple syrup and chocolate were early products that led to more complex methods of food processing. The sap from maple and other trees was made into syrup and sugar. And as technology evolved, so did the potential for new products and ingredients.

In the midst of these advancements, products native to other areas of the world—like Asia, Africa, and the Mediterranean—also entered the Americas and contributed to the expansion of food options. When Europeans arrived in the Americas, they further added to the diversity of food. They also introduced their own culinary traditions. Vice versa, when their visit to the Americas concluded, they took back to Europe some foods and recipes that they discovered overseas.

This culinary exchange helps explain why one continent can vary so greatly in its cuisine from region to region. Some areas may continue enhancing their own indigenous dishes while others are influenced by incoming foreign cultures. One clear example of this is South America. In its northern nations, popular food items point out the influence of Spanish culture. Meanwhile, just a couple borders away, Brazil's cuisine exemplifies some Portuguese traditions.

To this day, food and recipes continue to evolve throughout North and South America. From ingredients to methods and equipment, the culinary world is a hybrid of tradition and modernization, resulting in deliciously diverse opportunities to taste and experience.

ONCE UPON A PESTO

CHAPTER 1: NATIVE AMERICAN
Pumpkin Pesto
INSPIRED BY NATIVE AMERICANS

FOLK or FAIRY — SAVORY

MAKES 2 CUPS

TELLTALE and TIME — BEGINNER — 2 MINUTES

Jessica Paholsky

Pumpkins are part of the squash family. Well before the pilgrims arrived in North America, pumpkin was a staple in Indian diets. Its uses ranged from soups to desserts. And both the flesh and seeds of pumpkin were important elements within meals. Native Americans introduced pumpkin and other foods to immigrants in the 1500s when they arrived in North America.

INGREDIENTS

1/4 cup shelled pecans

2 cups pumpkin puree (fresh or canned)

1/4 cup (or 2 ounces) cream cheese

2 tablespoons maple syrup

1/2 teaspoon ground cardamom

DIRECTIONS

1. Combine all of the ingredients in a food processor. Blend until the desired consistency forms.

2. If using a mortar and pestle, crush the pecans until a fine crumb forms. Add the pumpkin puree and mash until smooth. Mix in the remaining ingredients. Mash until the desired consistency forms.

3. Store pesto in an airtight container or jar in the refrigerator for up to one week. Use throughout the week in the next two recipes. Pesto can last in an airtight container in the freezer for up to six months.

Once Upon a Pesto

Pumpkin is said to have originated in North America. Its name comes from a Greek word meaning 'large melon.'

ONCE UPON A PESTO

Stuffed Turkey Meatloaf

MADE WITH PUMPKIN PESTO

MAKES 4 TO 6 SERVINGS

TELLTALE *and* TIME

ADVANCED

1 HOUR AND 20 MINUTES

JESSICA PAHOLSKY

Poyha is a Cherokee tribe recipe similar to meatloaf. It traditionally calls for venison. However, turkey is an important protein source for Native Americans, who started raising turkeys about ten centuries ago. They used turkeys for their feathers before they started using them for food.

INGREDIENTS

For the meat:
1 1/3 pounds ground turkey
1/3 cup oatmeal
1/4 cup chopped onion
1 tablespoon chopped carrots
1 egg
1/2 teaspoon ground sage
salt and pepper to taste

For the filling:
1 cup cooked potatoes, peeled and mashed
1/3 cup Pumpkin Pesto
1/4 cup (or 2 ounces) cream cheese

DIRECTIONS

1. Heat oven to 350° F.
2. In a medium-size mixing bowl, combine the ingredients for the meat. Mix lightly just until incorporated. Set aside.
3. In a small mixing bowl, combine the ingredients for the filling. Mix together with a beater until smooth.
4. On a greased surface, flatten the meat mixture into a rectangle about 1/2 inch thick. Scoop the potato mixture onto the center of the meat rectangle, leaving about 2 inches exposed on each side. Wrap the edges of the meat up and over the potatoes. Seal the seams of the meat by gently pinching. This should form a log.
5. Transfer to a 9-by-13-inch pan.
6. Bake for 50 minutes to 1 hour, or until the outside begins to turn golden brown and slightly shiny.
7. Let cool for at least 5 minutes before slicing and serving.

Once Upon a Pesto

The Incas of South America most likely made the first version of mashed potatoes, but they didn't use butter, cream, or milk in their recipe.

Just Right

The meatloaf ingredients need only be lightly mixed with your hands until combined. Avoid over-mixing, or stirring too long with a spoon or fork.

Cranberry Nausamp

MADE WITH PUMPKIN PESTO

MAKES 4 TO 6 SERVINGS

TELLTALE and TIME
INTERMEDIATE — 20 MINUTES

Jessica Paholsky

Nausamp is one traditional Native American dish. Sometimes simply called *samp*, it's a Wampanoag recipe that includes dried corn, local berries, and nuts. Think of it as a porridge, which is boiled over heat until it thickens.

INGREDIENTS

1 cup cornmeal

2/3 cup chopped fresh cranberries

1/3 cup pumpkin seeds

3 cups water

3/4 cup Pumpkin Pesto

1/4 cup maple syrup

pinch of salt

DIRECTIONS

1. In a medium-size pot over medium-high heat, combine all of the ingredients. Bring to a boil.

2. Reduce the heat and simmer for 10 to 12 minutes, stirring often.

3. Let cool for 3 minutes before serving. Or let cool completely, then slice and bake or pan-fry for a crispier and more portable nausamp.

Once Upon a Pesto

The traditional process of making *nausamp* involves preparing the corn. Much like the earliest forms of pesto, corn was ground using tools like a mortar and pestle.

Just Right

The best way to achieve a smooth porridge is to stir constantly. Adding a pinch of salt to the porridge helps bring out the sweetness of the cranberries.

ONCE UPON A PESTO

CHAPTER 2: MAYAN
Mushroom and Chia Pesto
INSPIRED BY THE MAYANS

FOLK *or* FAIRY — NUT-FREE, SAVORY

MAKES 2 CUPS

TELLTALE *and* TIME — BEGINNER, 2 MINUTES

JESSICA PAHOLSKY

Mushrooms and chia seeds are important in Mayan culture and beliefs. Ancient Mayan people believed mushrooms created psychedelic effects. They also thought chia seeds possessed supernatural powers and used them in religious practices. In Mayan, the word chia means 'strength.' Chia seeds are tiny, but touted for providing stamina to warriors.

INGREDIENTS

- 1 tablespoon chia seeds
- 2 cups chopped mixed fresh mushrooms
- 1 loosely-packed cup fresh basil
- 1/3 cup fresh mozzarella cheese
- 1/2 tablespoon honey
- 1/4 cup olive oil

DIRECTIONS

1. Combine all of the ingredients in a food processor. Blend until the desired consistency forms.

2. If using a mortar and pestle, crush the chia seeds until a fine crumb forms. Add the mushrooms and basil, and mash until smooth. Mix in the remaining ingredients. Mash until the desired consistency forms.

3. Store pesto in an airtight container or jar in the refrigerator for up to one week. Use throughout the week in the next two recipes. Pesto can last in an airtight container in the freezer for up to six months.

Once Upon a Pesto

Mushroom motifs have been found on Mayan temple ruins, indicating the significance of this ingredient in the rich history of Mesoamerican civilization.

ONCE UPON A PESTO

Tamale Cups

MADE WITH MUSHROOM AND CHIA PESTO

MAKES 1 DOZEN CUPS

TELLTALE *and* TIME
ADVANCED — 35 MINUTES

JESSICA PAHOLSKY

Mayan *tamales* are portable servings of a starch encasing a protein-based filling. They play an important role in the cuisine of Mayan people. They are traditionally wrapped in corn husks or banana leaves, and then steamed. Some Mayan *tamales* feature turkey or iguana.

INGREDIENTS

2 cups masa flour

1 teaspoon baking powder

1 teaspoon salt

1 1/2 cups vegetable broth

1/4 cup butter, softened

1 16-ounce can black beans, drained and rinsed

1 large handful spinach, wilted in a pan over low heat

1/3 cup Mushroom and Chia Pesto

pinch each of paprika, cumin, cayenne, salt, and pepper

12 pieces fresh mozzarella cheese

DIRECTIONS

1. Heat oven to 350° F.
2. In a large bowl, combine masa flour, baking powder, and salt. Stir. Add vegetable broth, and stir until a spongy dough forms. Fold in butter until incorporated. Work the dough for 1 minute.
3. Grease a large 12-cup muffin tin. Divide the dough into 12 balls. Place each ball into one cup of the muffin tin (for easier removal, use cupcake liners instead of greasing). Press the dough along the bottom and sides of each cup. Set aside.
4. In a medium bowl, combine the black beans, spinach, Mushroom and Chia Pesto, and seasonings. Mash with a fork.
5. Scoop the black bean mixture into each dough cup, dividing evenly among the 12 cups.
6. Bury a piece of mozzarella cheese in the center of each cup, covering it with the surrounding black bean mixture.
7. Bake for 20 minutes, or until the edges of the corn mixture turn golden.
8. Let cool for 3 minutes before gently removing each tamale cup from the muffin tin.

Once Upon a Pesto

Tamales **are believed to have originated in Mesoamerica some 10,000 years ago.**

Just Right

Like traditional *tamale*-making, corn husks can be used to line the muffin tin instead of greasing it or using cupcake liners. It can be hard to find corn husks, but some grocery stores regularly keep them in stock. Specialized food stores can be more reliable sources.

ONCE UPON A PESTO

Salisbury Steak

MADE WITH MUSHROOM AND CHIA PESTO

MAKES 4 TO 6 SERVINGS

TELLTALE *and* TIME
ADVANCED — 40 MINUTES

Jessica Paholsky

American physician Dr. Salisbury is said to have invented this beef dish, and as a result, it was named Salisbury steak. Traditionally, Salisbury steak is served over mashed potatoes. Highlighting a Mayan starch that has a consistency comparable to potatoes, mashed plantains are substituted instead.

INGREDIENTS

For the mashed plantains:

3 green plantains, peeled and cut into 1-inch pieces
2 tablespoons butter
1/4 teaspoon cinnamon
1 cup milk

For the Salisbury steak:

1 pound ground beef
1/3 cup bread crumbs
1/4 teaspoon salt
1/8 teaspoon pepper
1 egg
1/2 teaspoon Dijon mustard
1 1/2 cups beef broth
1/2 cup Mushroom and Chia Pesto
3 tablespoons flour
1 tablespoon butter

DIRECTIONS

1. In a medium pan over low heat, combine plantains, butter, and cinnamon. Cover and cook for 15 minutes. Stir often to prevent browning.

2. Meanwhile, in a medium bowl, combine beef, bread crumbs, salt, pepper, egg, and Dijon. Mix until incorporated. Divide the mixture into 12 meatballs.

3. In a large pan over medium-high heat, add the meatballs. Cook for 10 minutes, tossing every 2 to 3 minutes to prevent overcooking any one side.

4. In another medium bowl, combine the broth, Mushroom and Chia Pesto, and flour. Stir to incorporate. Add the broth mixture and butter to the pan with the meatballs. Stir to coat the meatballs with the gravy. Cover and reduce the heat to a simmer. Cook for 15 minutes. Stir occasionally.

5. While the gravy and meatballs cook, prepare the mashed plantains. Transfer the cooked plantain pieces to a large mixing bowl. Add the milk and mix to the desired smoothness.

6. When the meatballs and gravy finish cooking, scoop and divide the mashed plantains among serving plates. Top with meatballs and gravy.

Once Upon a Pesto

Mayan breakfast is said to include plantains and rich coffee. This is similar to modern American breakfasts, which sometimes include bananas, a cousin of plantains.

Just Right

Original recipes for Salisbury steak include a bed of mashed potatoes or mashed peas. One cup of thawed green peas can be added in step 5 to mimic this tradition.

CHAPTER 3: SOUTHERN UNITED STATES

Collard Greens Pesto

INSPIRED BY SOUTHERN UNITED STATES

FOLK or FAIRY — DAIRY-FREE, SAVORY

MAKES 1 CUP

TELLTALE and TIME — BEGINNER, 2 MINUTES

Jessica Paholsky

A staple in Southern cooking, collard greens have a history even deeper than that part of the United States. Call them the dinosaurs of the vegetable family because they trace their roots to prehistoric times. Some say collards found their way from Africa to America. Since then, the leafy green has become a common ingredient in typical recipes of the South.

INGREDIENTS

- 1/4 cup shelled pecans
- 6 ounces collard greens
- 2 garlic cloves, peeled
- 1/2 teaspoon paprika
- 1/8 teaspoon cayenne
- 1 teaspoon dried oregano
- 1/8 teaspoon salt
- 1/4 cup olive oil
- 2 tablespoons honey

DIRECTIONS

1. Combine all of the ingredients in a food processor. Blend until the desired consistency forms.

2. If using a mortar and pestle, crush the pecans until a fine crumb forms. Add the collard greens and garlic, and mash until smooth. Mix in the remaining ingredients. Mash until the desired consistency forms.

3. Store pesto in an airtight container or jar in the refrigerator for up to one week. Use throughout the week in the next two recipes. Pesto can last in an airtight container in the freezer for up to six months.

Once Upon a Pesto

In the South, people eat collard greens and cornbread on New Year's Day to ensure a prosperous year ahead.

ONCE UPON A PESTO

Deviled Eggs

MADE WITH COLLARD GREENS PESTO

MAKES 12 SERVINGS

TELLTALE *and* TIME
INTERMEDIATE — 10 MINUTES

JESSICA PAHOLSKY

Deviled eggs are closely tied to the South, but their roots are not American. They were first served as an appetizer in ancient Rome. The name deviled eggs and the dish's ingredients evolved over time as more people began making their own versions of the recipe.

INGREDIENTS

6 hard-boiled eggs, peeled and cut in half lengthwise

3 tablespoons mayonnaise

2 tablespoons Collard Greens Pesto

1/2 teaspoon Dijon mustard

2 slices bacon, cooked and crumbled into small pieces

*optional: paprika for garnish

DIRECTIONS

1. Remove the egg yolks from each hard-boiled egg half, and transfer them to a small mixing bowl. Place each empty egg white half on a serving dish.

2. In the bowl with the egg yolks, add the mayonnaise, Collard Greens Pesto, and Dijon. Mash with a fork until blended together and smooth.

3. Transfer the yolk mixture to a Ziploc bag and seal the bag shut. With scissors, cut off a 1/4-inch corner of the bag. Squeeze out the filling into the bowl of each egg white half.

4. Sprinkle bacon pieces over each deviled egg.

5. Serve, or refrigerate for up to five days in an airtight container.

Once Upon a Pesto

Other names for deviled eggs include eggs mimosa, stuffed eggs, and Russian eggs. Many variants of deviled eggs exist internationally.

Just Right

To devil means to mix with a hot or spicy ingredient. For additional heat, add a pinch of red pepper flakes or a couple drops of Tabasco sauce to the egg yolk mixture during step 2.

ONCE UPON A PESTO

Succotash

MADE WITH COLLARD GREENS PESTO

MAKES 8 TO 12 SERVINGS

TELLTALE *and* TIME

BEGINNER — 10 MINUTES

JESSICA PAHOLSKY

Succotash is a classic side dish at Thanksgiving in New England and in the South alike. It's made with corn, lima beans, and lard. Some people prefer to modify the recipe by replacing lard with an alternative ingredient, such as olive oil or vegetable stock.

INGREDIENTS

1 15.5-ounce can corn, drained and rinsed

1 15.5-ounce can butter beans, drained and rinsed

1 15.5-ounce can black-eyed peas, drained and rinsed

1 12-ounce bag frozen lima beans, thawed

2 tablespoons Collard Greens Pesto

2 tablespoons olive oil

2 tablespoons apple cider vinegar

1 tablespoon honey

DIRECTIONS

1. In a large mixing bowl, combine the corn, butter beans, black-eyed peas, and lima beans.

2. In a small dish, whisk together the Collard Greens Pesto, olive oil, vinegar, and honey.

3. Immediately before serving, drizzle vinaigrette over corn and beans. Gently toss to coat.

Once Upon a Pesto

In cold seasons, this recipe can be turned into a hot dish by mixing the corn, butter beans, black-eyed peas, and lima beans in a pan over medium-high heat instead of in a large mixing bowl, heating for 8 to 10 minutes.

Just Right

Msickquatash, which is a Native American word for 'boiled corn,' is thought to be a forerunner to succotash as well as the source for its modern name.

CHAPTER 4: THE MIDWEST UNITED STATES

Pecan Pesto

INSPIRED BY THE MIDWEST UNITED STATES

FOLK or FAIRY — SAVORY

MAKES 2 CUPS

TELLTALE and TIME — BEGINNER — 2 MINUTES

JESSICA PAHOLSKY

Butternut squash and pecans are both native to North America. Pecans trace their origins to the state of Oklahoma. In fact, it's recorded that Thomas Jefferson gave George Washington pecan trees from the Midwest at his home in Virginia.

INGREDIENTS

1/4 cup shelled pecans

2 cups cooked butternut squash (cubed)

1/3 cup fresh sage

1/3 cup gorgonzola cheese

1/2 teaspoon salt

2 tablespoons olive oil

DIRECTIONS

1. Combine all of the ingredients in a food processor. Blend until the desired consistency forms.

2. If using a mortar and pestle, crush the pecans until a fine crumb forms. Add the butternut squash and sage, and mash until smooth. Mix in the remaining ingredients. Mash until the desired consistency forms.

3. Store pesto in an airtight container or jar in the refrigerator for up to one week. Use throughout the week in the next two recipes. Pesto can last in an airtight container in the freezer for up to six months.

Once Upon a Pesto

A few states in the United States account for nearly half of the world's production of pecans. These states include Georgia, New Mexico, and Texas.

ONCE UPON A PESTO

35

Kale Salad

MADE WITH PECAN PESTO

MAKES 6 SERVINGS

TELLTALE and TIME
ADVANCED — 1 HOUR AND 30 MINUTES

JESSICA PAHOLSKY

Kale has become a popular superfood across the United States, and that popularity has skyrocketed in the Midwest. What has already been and still remains popular in the Midwest is cornbread, which can be turned into slightly sweet and crunchy croutons.

INGREDIENTS

1 16-oz. bag of fresh kale
1 cup pomegranate seeds

For the cornbread croutons:
1/2 cup cornmeal
1/2 cup flour
2 tablespoons brown sugar
2 teaspoons baking powder
1/2 teaspoon salt
1/2 cup plus 1 tablespoon water

For the vinaigrette:
1/2 cup Pecan Pesto
1/4 cup olive oil
1/4 cup apple cider vinegar

DIRECTIONS

1. Heat oven to 425° F.
2. In a medium mixing bowl, combine the cornmeal, flour, brown sugar, baking powder, salt, and water. Stir until a smooth mixture forms.
3. Grease an 8-inch square baking dish and pour in the cornbread mixture.
4. Bake for 20 minutes, or until golden brown around the edges. Remove and let cool for 30 minutes.
5. Reduce the oven to 350° F.
6. Cut the cornbread into 1-inch cubes and spread evenly on a cookie sheet. Bake for another 30 minutes, or until croutons are crunchy on the outside.
7. Meanwhile in a small dish, combine the Pecan Pesto, olive oil, and apple cider vinegar.
8. Loosely chop the kale and transfer to a large serving bowl.
9. Pour the vinaigrette over the kale and toss to incorporate. Gently fold in the pomegranate seeds.
10. Remove the cornbread croutons from the oven. Top the salad with the croutons and serve.

Once Upon a Pesto

Midwestern cornbread differs from other regions' cornbread in the cornmeal-to-flour ratio. The ratio used in the Midwest creates a more airy texture.

Just Right

Some traditional Midwestern recipes for cornbread call for molasses as the sweetener. Replace the brown sugar with 1 tablespoon of molasses for this traditional style.

ONCE UPON A PESTO

Crispy Gnocchi

MADE WITH PECAN PESTO

MAKES 8 SERVINGS

TELLTALE *and* TIME
INTERMEDIATE — 25 MINUTES

JESSICA PAHOLSKY

Italian immigrants tend to populate urban America, including Midwestern cities like Chicago, Illinois and Cleveland, Ohio. In the Midwest, a popular cooking technique is frying. This ranges from fried chicken and cheese curds to Italian *gnocchi*.

INGREDIENTS

2 cups peeled, boiled russet potatoes (packed)

2 cups flour

1 egg

1/2 cup Pecan Pesto

4 tablespoons butter

DIRECTIONS

1. Over medium-high heat, bring a large pot of water to a boil.

2. Meanwhile, in a large mixing bowl, mix the potatoes, flour, egg, and Pecan Pesto until a smooth, firm dough forms.

3. Divide the dough into 4 parts and round each part into a ball. Dust the counter with flour and roll each dough ball into a snake, about 1 to 1 1/2 inches in diameter.

4. Cut the dough snake every inch to form rectangular pillows. Sprinkle more flour over them to prevent sticking.

5. Freeze the gnocchi for up to several months, then thaw before preparing. Or prepare fresh.

6. When preparing the gnocchi, add them to a large pot of boiling water. Boil for about 5 minutes, or until they begin to float. Drain the pot of water completely and set aside.

7. In a large pan, heat the butter over medium-high until melted, about 1 minute. Stir the butter until it begins to brown, about 3 minutes.

8. Add the cooked gnocchi to the pan. Cook, stirring occasionally, until golden brown, about 5 minutes. Remove from the heat and serve.

Once Upon a Pesto

Many Italian immigrants settled in the Midwest during the 19th century. Illinois, in particular, appealed to them because it offered opportunities for steady work. During that time, Chicago was the Midwest's leading industrial center.

Just Right

An alternative cooking method to boiling and frying *gnocchi* is roasting them. This method makes a more dense texture, and it still results in a crispy and browned exterior.

CHAPTER 5: NEW YORK
Green Bean Pesto
INSPIRED BY NEW YORK

FOLK *or* FAIRY — SAVORY

MAKES 1¾ CUPS

TELLTALE *and* TIME — BEGINNER — 2 MINUTES

Jessica Paholsky

A native of New York, Calvin Keeney earned the title Father of the Stringless Bean during the mid-19th century when he developed a bean that was less tough and fibrous. He tended over 6,000 acres of peas and beans, and also developed 19 different types of snap beans.

INGREDIENTS

1/2 cup shelled almonds

2 cups fresh green beans cut into 1-inch pieces

1/2 cup freshly grated Parmigiano Reggiano cheese

2 garlic cloves, peeled

1 tablespoon Dijon mustard

3 tablespoons sesame oil

2 tablespoons water

1/4 teaspoon ground black pepper

DIRECTIONS

1. Combine all of the ingredients in a food processor. Blend until the desired consistency forms.

2. If using a mortar and pestle, crush the almonds until a crumb forms. Add the green beans, Parmigiano Reggiano cheese, and garlic, and mash until smooth. Mix in the remaining ingredients. Mash until the desired consistency forms.

3. Store pesto in an airtight container or jar in the refrigerator for up to one week. Use throughout the week in the next two recipes. Pesto can last in an airtight container in the freezer for up to six months.

Once Upon a Pesto

Calvin Keeney's accomplishments in the bean world climaxed when Burpee Seeds commercially released a stringless green pod in 1894.

ONCE UPON A PESTO

Reuben Pizza

MADE WITH GREEN BEAN PESTO

MAKES 8 SERVINGS

TELLTALE and TIME
ADVANCED
1 HOUR AND 30 MINUTES

JESSICA PAHOLSKY

New York pizza is known for its crust. And the Reuben sandwich is a staple in New York delis. But, unknown is how this sandwich got its name. It could have been New York restaurant owner and German immigrant Arnold Reuben. Or it could have been Reuben Kulakofsky in Omaha, Nebraska.

INGREDIENTS

For the dough:
2 1/2 teaspoons active dry yeast
1/2 cup warm water
1/2 teaspoon sugar
1/2 teaspoon salt
1 tablespoon olive oil
1 1/2 cups all-purpose flour

For the sauce:
3 tablespoons mayonnaise
1/4 cup Green Bean Pesto

For the pizza:
6 slices Swiss cheese
1 cup drained sauerkraut
3 slices pastrami or corned beef
3/4 cup shredded mozzarella cheese

DIRECTIONS

1. For the dough, combine the yeast and warm water in a large mixing bowl. Let sit for 5 minutes, or until foamy.

2. Mix in the sugar, salt, and olive oil. Add the flour and knead for 4 minutes, or until smooth and leathery.

3. Transfer the dough to a lightly greased bowl and cover it with a damp towel. Let rise in a warm place for 45 minutes, or until doubled in size.

4. Heat oven to 425° F.

5. Roll out the dough into a 12-inch pizza crust on a pizza stone or a lightly greased cookie sheet.

6. In a small mixing bowl, stir together the sauce ingredients. Spread evenly onto the pizza crust with the backside of a spoon.

7. Top the pizza with a layer each of Swiss cheese, sauerkraut, pastrami or corned beef, and mozzarella cheese.

8. Bake for 20 minutes, or until the crust is cooked through and the cheese turns slightly golden.

9. Let cool for 5 minutes before slicing and serving.

Once Upon a Pesto

Italian immigrants largely influenced pizza in New York. With their recipes from Naples fresh in mind, both Neapolitan and New York-style pizzas use thinner crusts.

Just Right

If you're tight on time, use a store-bought pizza crust and start at step 4. Reduce the baking time, as necessary, so the crust does not burn.

Chef Salad

MADE WITH GREEN BEAN PESTO

MAKES 1 SERVING

TELLTALE *and* TIME

BEGINNER — 10 MINUTES

The chef who invented the Chef Salad is debatable. Some say it was Chef Diat. Others say Chef Seydoux or Chef Roser. What's the common thread? All three chefs worked during the 20th century in New York hotels, making the salad's geographic origin pretty clear.

INGREDIENTS

For the dressing:

2 tablespoons Green Bean Pesto

2 tablespoons mayonnaise

1 tablespoon honey

For the salad:

3 cups chopped Romaine lettuce

1/2 cup cucumber slices

1/2 tomato, sliced

1 hard-boiled egg, sliced

1/4 cup shredded cheddar cheese

1-2 slices honey ham, cut into 1/2-inch-thick pieces

1-2 slices turkey breast, cut into 1/2-inch-thick pieces

DIRECTIONS

1. In a small mixing bowl, stir together the dressing ingredients until incorporated. Set aside.

2. In a salad bowl or on a large plate, spread the lettuce. Top it with the cucumber, tomato, egg, cheddar cheese, ham, and turkey.

3. Drizzle the salad dressing on top, or serve it on the side.

Once Upon a Pesto

Chef Salad can trace its roots several centuries back in time. *Salmagundi* is a popular meat and salad dish that originated in England during the 17th century. It became widely popular in colonial America, and it seems to be a predecessor of today's Chef Salad.

CHAPTER 6: CANADA
Maple Syrup Pesto
INSPIRED BY CANADA

FOLK *or* FAIRY
DAIRY-FREE, SAVORY

MAKES 1 ¾ CUPS

TELLTALE *and* TIME
BEGINNER — 2 MINUTES

46

JESSICA PAHOLSKY

The maple leaf is almost synonymous with Canada. The image of a maple leaf is big, red, and central on Canada's flag. This iconography was also used in 1868 on the coat of arms of both Quebec and Ontario. In terms of its literal name, "The Maple Leaf Forever" is the title of a Canadian song that became English-speaking Canada's unofficial anthem. And last, but not least, Canada produces about three-quarters of the world's pure maple syrup.

INGREDIENTS

1/4 cup shelled pecans

2 cups peeled and cut raw acorn squash

1/4 cup 100% pure maple syrup

1/4 teaspoon ground nutmeg

1/2 teaspoon ground ginger

1 teaspoon vanilla

DIRECTIONS

1. Combine all of the ingredients in a food processor. Blend until the desired consistency forms.

2. If using a mortar and pestle, crush the pecans until a fine crumb forms. Add the acorn squash and mash until smooth. Mix in the remaining ingredients. Mash until the desired consistency forms.

3. Store pesto in an airtight container or jar in the refrigerator for up to one week. Use throughout the week in the next two recipes. Pesto can last in an airtight container in the freezer for up to six months.

Once Upon a Pesto

Maple syrup production began in Canada during the 18th century when indigenous people taught European settlers techniques to harvest sap. Over time, producers improved these techniques to make larger-scale production possible.

ONCE UPON A PESTO

Bacon Monkey Bread

MADE WITH MAPLE SYRUP PESTO

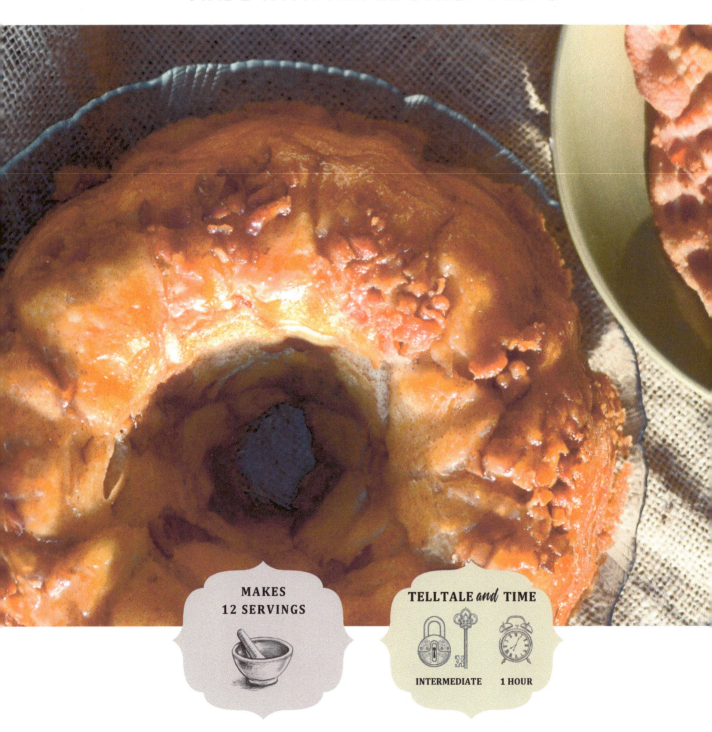

MAKES 12 SERVINGS

TELLTALE *and* TIME

INTERMEDIATE — 1 HOUR

JESSICA PAHOLSKY

In Canada, there's no such thing as Canadian bacon. The term is used because when there was a shortage of pork in the United Kingdom during the 19th century, pork was imported from Canada. Canadian bacon is made from the lean eye of the loin, whereas other bacon comes from the pig's belly.

INGREDIENTS

1/2 cup butter

1/3 cup brown sugar

3/4 cup Maple Syrup Pesto

1/2 cup sugar

1 1/2 teaspoons ground cinnamon

10 slices bacon, cooked and crumbled (reserve bacon grease)

2 16-ounce tubes biscuit dough, removed from casing and cut into quarters

DIRECTIONS

1. Heat oven to 350° F.
2. In a small saucepan over medium heat, melt the butter. Add the brown sugar, and stir until dissolved. Stir in the Maple Syrup Pesto until combined. Remove from the heat and set aside.
3. In a small bowl, combine the sugar and cinnamon.
4. To prepare the biscuit dough, dip one side of each piece into the reserved bacon grease, then toss in the cinnamon-sugar mixture to coat lightly.
5. In a greased Bundt pan, sprinkle 1/3 of crumbled bacon, then half of the prepared biscuit dough, then 1/3 of the bacon, then the remaining biscuit dough, and finally the remaining bacon.
6. Drizzle the pesto-butter mixture over the top.
7. Bake for 40 minutes.
8. Remove from the oven and let cool for 10 minutes. Invert the bread onto a large plate and serve warm, or keep refrigerated for up to one week.

Once Upon a Pesto

In Canada, peameal bacon or back bacon would be the equivalent of Canadian bacon because those products are made using the lean loin of the pig's back.

Just Right

If you don't have a traditional Bundt pan, you can make monkey bread in a greased bread pan, ramekin, or loaf pan. Just be sure to maintain an even thickness so it cooks evenly throughout.

Rum Milkshake

MADE WITH MAPLE SYRUP PESTO

MAKES 1 SERVING

TELLTALE *and* TIME

BEGINNER — 5 MINUTES

JESSICA PAHOLSKY

One of Canada's most popular alcoholic drinks pairs rum and maple syrup with mulled wine. This drink, called *Caribou*, is often served at Quebec's Winter Carnival. Not too far away, Nova Scotia is considered rum country. Distilling rum actually preceded building ships in this maritime province.

INGREDIENTS

1/2 cup Maple Syrup Pesto

1 cup vanilla ice cream

1/4 cup milk

3 tablespoons rum

DIRECTIONS

1. Combine all of the ingredients in a blender or food processor. Blend until smooth.

2. Pour into a serving glass.

3. Top with whipped cream and a maraschino cherry, if desired.

Once Upon a Pesto

During World War I, soldiers believed rum provided physical and mental health benefits. Canadian soldiers particularly saw value in this beverage during cold, wet nights.

Just Right

For a non-alcoholic version, simply don't add rum.

CHAPTER 7: PUERTO RICO
Passion Fruit Pesto
INSPIRED BY PUERTO RICO

FOLK or FAIRY — DAIRY-FREE, SWEET

MAKES 1 CUP

TELLTALE and TIME — BEGINNER, 2 MINUTES

Jessica Paholsky

In Puerto Rico, passion fruit is known as *parcha*. It's often used in juices, ice cream, and pastries. Passion fruit can be found in many tropical countries, and it consists of a rind that encases about 250 seeds, which are each surrounded by membranes of acidic juice.

INGREDIENTS

1/2 cup shelled cashews

flesh of 3 passion fruit

1/2 cara cara orange with rind, plus 1 tablespoon juice

3/4 cup chopped fresh basil

1/2 teaspoon ground ginger

1 tablespoon honey

DIRECTIONS

1. Combine all of the ingredients in a food processor. Blend until the desired consistency forms.

2. If using a mortar and pestle, crush the cashews until a fine crumb forms. Add the passion fruit, cara cara orange, and basil, and mash until smooth. Mix in the remaining ingredients. Mash until the desired consistency forms.

3. Store pesto in an airtight container or jar in the refrigerator for up to one week. Use throughout the week in the next two recipes. Pesto can last in an airtight container in the freezer for up to six months.

Once Upon a Pesto

The name passion fruit dates back to the fruit's origins in South America, specifically in Brazil. The passion fruit flower appears in some religious drawings, and priests recognized the plant as a symbol for Christ's Passion.

ONCE UPON A PESTO

Caribbean Coleslaw with Mango

MADE WITH PASSION FRUIT PESTO

MAKES 8 TO 12 SERVINGS

TELLTALE and TIME
BEGINNER — 10 MINUTES

JESSICA PAHOLSKY

Cabbage is one of the most widely used vegetables in Latin American countries. Mango is also a popular ingredient in Puerto Rican cooking. Even though mango is not indigenous to this island nation, mango trees line Puerto Rico's roadsides and sometimes grow up to 40 feet tall.

INGREDIENTS

1/2 savoy cabbage, shredded

1/2 white cabbage, shredded

1/3 red onion, thinly sliced

1 mango, cut into 1-inch-long sticks

2 tablespoons apple cider vinegar

1/2 cup Passion Fruit Pesto

4 tablespoons mayonnaise

4 teaspoons sugar

1/4 teaspoon crushed red pepper

DIRECTIONS

1. In a large mixing bowl, toss together the cabbages, onion, and mango.

2. In a small mixing bowl, mix together the remaining ingredients. Whisk until incorporated. Then, pour the dressing over the cabbage mixture in the large bowl. Toss well.

3. Serve, or store in an airtight container in the refrigerator for up to 4 days.

Once Upon a Pesto

Across the Caribbean Sea from Puerto Rico in El Salvador, *curtido* is a coleslaw usually made with cabbage, carrot, onion, oregano, and vinegar.

Just Right

The secret to choosing the right mango is not in its color. Squeeze the mango gently and if it gives slightly, that means it's ripe.

Once Upon A Pesto

Piña Colada

MADE WITH PASSION FRUIT PESTO

MAKES 1 SERVING

TELLTALE *and* TIME

BEGINNER — 5 MINUTES

JESSICA PAHOLSKY

In 1978, Puerto Rico named piña colada its national beverage. This drink is said to have been first concocted in 1954 by Ramón Marrero, who then personally served the cocktail for the next 35 years while he bartended at a hotel in San Juan, the capital of Puerto Rico.

INGREDIENTS

1 cup ice cubes

2 tablespoons coconut cream

1/4 cup pineapple juice

2 tablespoons Passion Fruit Pesto

1/4 teaspoon cinnamon

1 teaspoon sugar

pineapple wedge for garnish

DIRECTIONS

1. In a blender or food processor, combine the ice, coconut cream, pineapple juice, and Passion Fruit Pesto. Blend until fairly smooth.

2. Mix together the cinnamon and sugar in a small bowl. Wet the top rim of a mason jar and dip the jar upside down into the cinnamon-sugar bowl, coating the rim lightly with the mixture.

3. Pour the blended piña colada into the mason jar.

4. Serve immediately with a pineapple wedge.

Once Upon a Pesto

When Ramón Marrero was commissioned to create the cocktail that became piña colada, it's said that it took him three months to come up with a final product.

Just Right

This piña colada is non-alcoholic. To make the drink alcoholic, add 1/4 cup of rum.

CHAPTER 8: PERU

Asparagus Pesto

INSPIRED BY PERU

FOLK or FAIRY — SAVORY

MAKES 2 CUPS

TELLTALE and TIME — BEGINNER — 2 MINUTES

JESSICA PAHOLSKY

Peru is among the world's largest producers of asparagus. Through irrigation methods, farmers in Peru are able to grow the stalk year round, and asparagus plants can produce for up to 15 to 20 years. Half of Peruvian asparagus crops are green asparagus, and the other half are white.

INGREDIENTS

1/3 cup shelled pistachios

3 cups 1-inch asparagus pieces (about 3/4 lb asparagus stalks)

1/2 cup diced sweet onion

3 tablespoons ricotta cheese

juice of 1/2 lemon

1/4 cup olive oil

1/4 teaspoon salt

1/4 teaspoon freshly ground black pepper

DIRECTIONS

1. Combine all of the ingredients in a food processor. Blend until the desired consistency forms.

2. If using a mortar and pestle, crush the cashews until a fine crumb forms. Add the passion fruit, cara cara orange, and basil, and mash until smooth. Mix in the remaining ingredients. Mash until the desired consistency forms.

3. Store pesto in an airtight container or jar in the refrigerator for up to one week. Use throughout the week in the next two recipes. Pesto can last in an airtight container in the freezer for up to six months.

Once Upon a Pesto

Asparagus is thought to have originated in the Mediterranean area. Today, the majority of the asparagus produced in Peru is sent to Europe, making the history and production of asparagus a complete circle.

ONCE UPON A PESTO

Quinoa Soup

MADE WITH ASPARAGUS PESTO

MAKES 8 TO 10 SERVINGS

TELLTALE and TIME

INTERMEDIATE, 35 MINUTES

JESSICA PAHOLSKY

Quinoa originated in the Andean region in and around Peru. As a protein-rich ancient grain in a nation where meat is sometimes scarce, it's a staple both on plates and in a classic bowl of soup.

INGREDIENTS

1/2 onion, sliced

3 garlic cloves, minced

1 tablespoon olive oil

1 cup frozen peas, thawed

2 cups butternut squash, cooked and cut into 1/2-inch cubes

2 cups cooked quinoa

2 cups cooked and chopped chicken breast

4 cups chicken stock

1/2 cup Asparagus Pesto

1 bay leaf

DIRECTIONS

1. In a medium-large pot over medium heat, sauté the onion and garlic in oil until the onion turns translucent, about 7 to 10 minutes.

2. Add the remaining ingredients to the pot and bring to a boil.

3. Reduce the heat to a simmer and cook for 20 minutes before serving.

Once Upon a Pesto

Quinoa was known as a crop for poor farmers until the late 20th century. When American researchers brought it to the United States, quinoa became known as a superfood, and demand for quinoa grew.

Just Right

If you have time, make this soup a day ahead of when you will be serving and eating it. Resting soup allows the proteins to break down for greater flavor. Just reheat the soup in a medium-large pot on the stovetop before serving.

Once Upon A Pesto

Street Corn

MADE WITH ASPARAGUS PESTO

MAKES 1 SERVING

TELLTALE *and* TIME

INTERMEDIATE, 35 MINUTES

Jessica Paholsky

Choclo is a variety of corn grown in the Andean Mountains of Peru. It's sweet and features large grains. It's common to find it topped with cheese and sold as street food in Peru.

INGREDIENTS

4 ears of sweet corn, husked

2 teaspoons olive oil

1 teaspoon ground cumin

1/2 cup Asparagus Pesto

1 oz goat cheese, crumbled

1 tablespoon chopped fresh parsley

DIRECTIONS

1. Warm a panini press to medium-high heat. Meanwhile, brush the corn cobs with olive oil and sprinkle with cumin.

2. Once the panini press is heated, place the corn cobs on the press. Cook, turning every 3 minutes, for about 25 to 30 minutes, or until light brown and charred in some areas.

3. Divide the Asparagus Pesto atop the corn cobs.

4. Sprinkle each corn cob with goat cheese and parsley.

Once Upon a Pesto

Choclo, or the sweet corn of Peru, is traditionally sold as street corn. It's also commonly served with Peru's famous *ceviche*, a dish made with raw fish cured in acidic juices.

Just Right

If you don't have access to a panini press, some other options for cooking corn cobs include grilling, boiling, or roasting in the oven at 425° F.

ONCE UPON A PESTO

CHAPTER 9: CHILE

Rhubarb Pesto

INSPIRED BY CHILE

FOLK *or* FAIRY
DAIRY-FREE, SAVORY

MAKES 1 CUP

TELLTALE *and* TIME
BEGINNER — 2 MINUTES

JESSICA PAHOLSKY

Rhubarb is a more recent addition in the produce world. One type of rhubarb, *gunnera tinctoria*, is native to Chile and called *nalca* there. Some know this species as Chilean prickly rhubarb, recognizing the attributes of the plant's very large leaves and thorny stem. Like other areas of the world, in Chile rhubarb stalks are often cooked in jams and other recipes.

INGREDIENTS

1/4 cup shelled walnuts

1 cup rhubarb pieces (cut into 1-inch pieces)

1 fennel bulb, chopped

1/2 cup chopped fresh mint

2 tablespoons caramel sauce

DIRECTIONS

1. Combine all of the ingredients in a food processor. Blend until the desired consistency forms.

2. If using a mortar and pestle, crush the walnuts until a fine crumb forms. Add the rhubarb, fennel, and mint, and mash until smooth. Mix in the caramel sauce. Mash until the desired consistency forms.

3. Store pesto in an airtight container or jar in the refrigerator for up to one week. Use throughout the week in the next two recipes. Pesto can last in an airtight container in the freezer for up to six months.

Once Upon a Pesto

Before it reached the Americas, rhubarb is believed to be a native plant of Serbia, where it was found growing along a river bank.

ONCE UPON A PESTO

Chili

MADE WITH RHUBARB PESTO

MAKES 6 SERVINGS

TELLTALE *and* TIME

INTERMEDIATE, 20 MINUTES

JESSICA PAHOLSKY

Chile with an "e" is a South American nation that runs along the Pacific Ocean. On the other hand, chili with an "i" is a stew typically made with ground beef, beans, tomatoes, and chili peppers. There are various theories on the etymology for the country Chile, but there are no known ties to its edible homophone.

INGREDIENTS

1 pound ground beef

1 cup chopped onion

1 cup chopped green bell peppers

1 28-ounce can crushed tomatoes

1 cup chopped McIntosh apple

1 15-ounce can pinto beans

1/3 cup Rhubarb Pesto

1/2 teaspoon ground cinnamon

1/4 teaspoon chili powder

1/4 teaspoon salt

DIRECTIONS

1. In a medium-large pot over medium-high heat, combine the beef, onion, and peppers. Cook, stirring occasionally, until the meat is no longer pink.

2. Add the remaining ingredients to the beef mixture, stirring to incorporate.

3. Bring to a boil. Then reduce the heat, cover, and simmer for 15 minutes before serving.

Once Upon a Pesto

One theory for the name Chile points to the sound of a local Chilean bird, the *trile*. Spelled out, the bird's warble is *cheele-cheele*.

Just Right

With so many variations, chili recipes often include secret ingredients. From a shot of bourbon to some cinnamon, coffee, or chocolate, they add extra depth to the chili's base of flavor.

ONCE UPON A PESTO

Sopaipillas

MADE WITH RHUBARB PESTO

MAKES 2 DOZEN

TELLTALE *and* TIME

ADVANCED, 30 MINUTES

JESSICA PAHOLSKY

Sopaipillas have been a Chilean culinary tradition since as early as 1726. There is no right or wrong time to eat these fried pastry bites, and people in Chile enjoy them topped with chili pepper sauce, mustard, or ketchup. When eaten for dessert, *sopaipillas* are served with a caramel-like sauce.

INGREDIENTS

- 2 cups flour, sifted
- 2 teaspoons baking powder
- 1 teaspoon salt
- 1/3 cup water
- 2 tablespoons coconut oil
- 1/4 cup Rhubarb Pesto
- 1/4 cup sugar
- 1 teaspoon cinnamon
- 1/3 cup oil for frying
- 1 pint strawberries, hulled and sliced

DIRECTIONS

1. In a large mixing bowl, combine the flour, baking powder, and salt. Mix together.
2. Add the water, coconut oil, and Rhubarb Pesto to the flour mixture. Stir until a smooth dough forms. You can begin to knead the dough with your hands as it becomes thick and firm.
3. Roll the dough out on a floured surface to about 1/2 inch thick. Cut the dough into 2-inch triangles.
4. In a medium bowl, combine the cinnamon and sugar. Set aside.
5. Heat the frying oil in a large saucepan over medium heat. Once the oil is hot, add 5 to 10 dough triangles to the pan at a time. Cook each triangle for 30 to 45 seconds per side, or until golden brown.
6. As soon as each triangle is cooked on both sides, remove them from the pan and gently toss each one in the bowl of cinnamon-sugar, coating each lightly on all sides.
7. Then transfer to a plate to cool slightly.
8. Repeat steps 5 through 7 until all of the dough triangles have been fried.
9. Top with strawberries before serving.

Once Upon a Pesto

In central Chile, the dough for *sopaipillas* is made with cooked ground pumpkin. In the south, the traditional recipe doesn't include pumpkin.

Just Right

In Chile, another common accompaniment for *sopaipillas* is avocado. Peel and cut into small pieces 1 avocado, and add that to the strawberry topping in this recipe.

ONCE UPON A PESTO

CHAPTER 10: BRAZIL
Pineapple Pesto
INSPIRED BY BRAZIL

FOLK or FAIRY — DAIRY-FREE, SWEET

MAKES 1 1/2 CUPS

TELLTALE and TIME — BEGINNER, 2 MINUTES

JESSICA PAHOLSKY

Pineapple is said to be indigenous to the area that is today Brazil. The native people then spread the fruit throughout South and Central America. Pineapple acquired the nickname *anana,* which means 'excellent fruit.' Nowadays, Brazil is one of the leading producers of pineapple.

INGREDIENTS

1/3 cup shelled Brazil nuts

2 cups cut fresh pineapple

1 cup fresh basil

1 teaspoon vanilla

1 teaspoon fresh lime juice

1/8 teaspoon salt

DIRECTIONS

1. Combine all of the ingredients in a food processor. Blend until the desired consistency forms.

2. If using a mortar and pestle, crush the Brazil nuts until a fine crumb forms. Add the pineapple and basil, and mash until smooth. Mix in the remaining ingredients. Mash until the desired consistency forms.

3. Store pesto in an airtight container or jar in the refrigerator for up to one week. Use throughout the week in the next two recipes. Pesto can last in an airtight container in the freezer for up to six months.

Once Upon a Pesto

When Christopher Columbus traveled to the New World a second time in 1493, he and his crew discovered *anana*. They thought this fruit—pineapple—resembled the shape of a pinecone and had a texture similar to apples.

ONCE UPON A PESTO

Citrus Ribs

MADE WITH PINEAPPLE PESTO

MAKES 4 SERVINGS

TELLTALE *and* TIME
INTERMEDIATE — 3 HOURS

Jessica Paholsky

At a Brazilian steakhouse, also known as a *churrascaria*, rounds and rounds of meat that's been cooked over a barbecue are served. The dining experience reflects the fireside roasts that *gaúchos*, or cowboys, in southern Brazil had centuries ago.

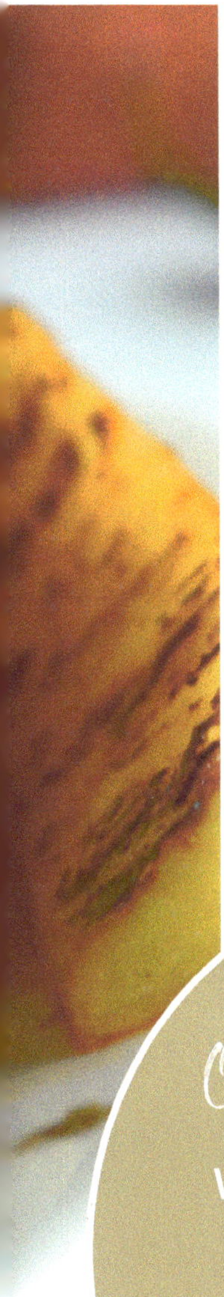

INGREDIENTS

1 pound boneless pork ribs

1/2 cup orange juice

2 cups beef broth

1 jalapeño, seeded and finely chopped

2 garlic cloves, minced

1/2 cup Pineapple Pesto

DIRECTIONS

1. In a medium pan over medium-high heat, brown the pork ribs, about 7 minutes per side.

2. Add the remaining ingredients to the pan and bring to a boil.

3. Reduce the heat to low. Cover and simmer for 2 1/2 hours. The meat should be tender and the sauce thickened.

Once Upon a Pesto

While *churrascaria* is the name for what we call a Brazilian steakhouse, *churrasco* is the process of preparing meats throughout Brazil.

Just Right

It's important to keep the pork ribs covered while cooking so they don't lose excess moisture.

Coffee Flan

MADE WITH PINEAPPLE PESTO

MAKES 2 SERVINGS

TELLTALE *and* TIME
ADVANCED — 1 DAY

Once Upon a Pesto

In Brazil, *pudim* refers to the preparation of a creamy—either sweet or savory—dish that is baked in a water bath.

JESSICA PAHOLSKY

Pudim, or pudding in English, may be better known as flan. This dessert is by far the most popular in Brazil, and the most popular drink in the nation is coffee. Not only is Brazil among the top coffee consumers in the world, but the country is also one of the beverage's leading global producers. in the Andean Mountains of Peru. It's sweet and features large grains. It's common to find it topped with cheese and sold as street food in Peru.

INGREDIENTS

3/4 cup, plus 1 tablespoon, water

1/4 cup, plus 2 tablespoons, sugar

1/4 cup Pineapple Pesto

1/2 teaspoon coffee grounds

6 egg yolks

DIRECTIONS

1. Heat oven to 350° F.
2. In a small saucepan over medium heat, combine 3/4 cup water, 2 tablespoons sugar, and Pineapple Pesto. Bring to a boil.
3. Cover and simmer for 25 minutes. Remove from the heat and let cool completely.
4. Meanwhile, in another small saucepan over low heat, combine 1 tablespoon water, 1/4 cup sugar, and coffee grounds. Cook until the sugar dissolves.
5. Increase the heat for the coffee mixture to high. Cook until amber in color.
6. Remove from heat. Transfer the small saucepan liquid to two 3/4-cup ramekins.
7. Once the pesto mixture has cooled, whisk in the egg yolks.
8. Divide the pesto and egg mixture between the two ramekins.
9. Add water to a pan large enough for the ramekins up to half the height of the ramekins. Then transfer the two ramekins to the pan.
10. Bake for 30 minutes. Let cool, and then cover.
11. Chill the cooled ramekins in the refrigerator overnight.
12. When ready to serve, gently slide a knife around the inside edges of each ramekin to loosen the flan. Place a small flat plate on top of the ramekin, flip to invert the flan, and then lift the ramekin directly upward to leave only the flan on the plate.

Just Right

Knowing when the flan is cooked completely is key to the success of making this dessert. A properly cooked flan won't jiggle in the middle.

ONCE UPON A PESTO

PART 2:
Europe

The history of food in Europe is uniquely rich and intriguingly eventful. Centuries ago, European culinary habits and ingredients created a launching pad for what is now considered a gastronomic hub of the world. If there's one continent where some travelers visit for the sole goal of food, it's Europe.

In ancient Greece and Rome, staple foods included vegetables, cereals and legumes, fruits, and cheese. Meat and fish were eaten, but mainly by higher classes. Cooking methods involved roasting, cooking, and boiling. And olives and grapes helped enhance various dishes. Those same olives and grapes were the cornerstone for agriculture, diet, and, eventually, processes like pressing to make olive oil and aging to make wine.

Sauce Similarity in Europe

Less than four hours by train or car from Liguria and the home of pesto Genovese, there's a similar-sounding green sauce in the Provence region of France. It's called **pistou.** Like its Italian neighbor, this sauce's key ingredients are basil, garlic, and olive oil. However, *pistou* doesn't include pine nuts or Parmigiano Reggiano cheese; those are Italian local specialties. *Pistou* is also most often used in a French soup called *soupe au pistou*, which is similar to minestrone. Every recipe can vary, but the key ingredients include legumes, vegetables, and grains.

The origins of this sauce's name are very similar to those of pesto. Italian and French are both Romance languages, which are all descendants of one form of Latin. Both Latin and Italian verbage include the word *pestare*, which means 'to pound' or' to crush.' The Italian word pesto comes from that Italian verb, and the French word *pistou* comes from a Latin homonym.

11. SPAIN
12. FRANCE
13. BELGIUM
14. SWEDEN
15. SWITZERLAND
16. ITALY
17. CROATIA
18. GREECE
19. CYPRUS
20. GEORGIA

With a mindful eye on these ingredients and processes, people in Europe started to record their culinary creations. In fact, the first known cookbook dates to the 5th century BC in Sicily. Not only did this book provide instruction, but it also planted seeds of inspiration during the Renaissance. People could now page through notes on foods and methods, and pass them on from generation to generation. Furthermore, written culinary records made it possible to bring lost traditions back to life. For example, foods like artichokes, capers, and olives were eaten during ancient times and then reinvigorated in Renaissance cooking.

During the Renaissance, cooking was artistic as much as it was practical, and certain foods took center stage. Most notably, vegetables became less prominent while meat became more distinguished. From its preparation to its table placement, meat was paired with herbs, spices, and sauces like never before. This was made possible, in part, by European traders returning from the Americas, Asia, and Africa with "new" foods. This ever-growing interest in cooking and the meal experience inspired hundreds more culinary texts.

Over the next couple of centuries, European culinary practices saw less evolution and more steadiness. However, at about the same time, the first breakaway occurred. The people of France decided to pave their own way in the food world when they discovered and incorporated new flavors and preparation methods. For example, they divided the meal experience into savory first, dessert last. They also brought vegetables back to light as the centerpiece in many recipes.

Following the French example, other cultures took to their own trendsetting, too. During the 19th and 20th centuries, restaurants, cookbooks, and food products developed a quality and quantity worthy of recognition. Global imports also sparked a new fascination for diversity and localization, allowing each culture, nation, and even household to redefine their own ingredient selection and cooking methods without forgetting their roots.

ONCE UPON A PESTO

CHAPTER 11: SPAIN
Red Cabbage Pesto
INSPIRED BY SPAIN

FOLK *or* FAIRY
NUT-FREE, DAIRY-FREE, SAVORY

MAKES 2 CUPS

TELLTALE *and* TIME
BEGINNER — 2 MINUTES

JESSICA PAHOLSKY

In Spain, Christmas Eve dinner usually includes a main entrée of seafood served with a red cabbage dish called *lombarda*. Throughout the country, it's made in different ways. For some, it's cooked with apples and smoky salt pork. Others add in potatoes, raisins, or pine nuts.

INGREDIENTS

2 1/2 cups chopped red cabbage

1/2 cup sliced water chestnuts

2 tablespoons honey

fresh juice of 1 lime

3 tablespoons olive oil

1/2 teaspoon crushed red pepper

DIRECTIONS

1. Combine all of the ingredients in a food processor. Blend until the desired consistency forms.

2. If using a mortar and pestle, mash the red cabbage and water chestnuts until smooth. Mix in the remaining ingredients. Mash until the desired consistency forms.

3. Store pesto in an airtight container or jar in the refrigerator for up to one week. Use throughout the week in the next two recipes. Pesto can last in an airtight container in the freezer for up to six months.

Once Upon a Pesto

Spain isn't the only country that includes red cabbage at Christmas time. Denmark also makes a similar dish. For both countries, the vegetable is easy to prepare and adds a festive color to the dinner table.

ONCE UPON A PESTO

Melon Gazpacho

MADE WITH RED CABBAGE PESTO

MAKES 4 SERVINGS

TELLTALE *and* TIME

BEGINNER — 5 MINUTES

JESSICA PAHOLSKY

Gazpacho is a cold soup typically made with blended raw tomatoes or other vegetables. It originated in Andalusia, a region in southern Spain. *Gazpacho* is especially popular as a cold dish because of the hot summers this region experiences.

INGREDIENTS

3 cucumbers (peeled, seeds removed, and chopped)

1/4 honeydew melon (peeled, seeds removed, and chopped)

1/4 cup Greek yogurt

1/2 cup Red Cabbage Pesto

DIRECTIONS

1. In a food processor, combine the cucumber, honeydew melon, and Greek yogurt. Blend until smooth.

2. Divide the mixture into four serving bowls.

3. Swirl in the Red Cabbage Pesto. Garnish with cucumber slivers and melon cubes as desired.

Once Upon a Pesto

Before *gazpacho* became a popular Spanish soup, it was an ancient Greek and Roman dish.

Just Right

The word *gazpacho* comes from the Arabic word for 'soaked bread.' Serve this gazpacho with croutons, if you wish.

Spanish Tortilla

MADE WITH RED CABBAGE PESTO

MAKES 4 TO 8 SERVINGS

TELLTALE *and* TIME

INTERMEDIATE, 45 MINUTES

Jessica Paholsky

More commonly known as a Spanish omelet, *tortilla española* is a dish made with eggs and potatoes. It can be served hot or cold and is one of many popular Spanish *tapas*, or small appetizers.

INGREDIENTS

1 cup uncooked pancetta

1/2 cup chopped onion

2 cups peeled, sliced sweet potatoes (1/8 inch thick)

4 tablespoons olive oil

6 eggs

1/2 cup Red Cabbage Pesto

salt and pepper to taste

DIRECTIONS

1. In a medium pan over high heat, cook the pancetta for 2 minutes.
2. Reduce the heat. Add the onion and cook for another 5 minutes, or until the onions become transparent. Remove from the heat. Set aside to cool.
3. In the same pan over medium heat, combine 2 tablespoons of olive oil and the sweet potato. Cook for 10 minutes, stirring continuously to keep potatoes from browning. Remove from the heat. Set aside to cool.
4. In a medium mixing bowl, whisk together the eggs and Red Cabbage Pesto. Add salt and pepper to taste.
5. Once the pancetta mixture and the sweet potato slices have cooled, gently add them to the egg mixture. Stir until incorporated.
6. In the medium pan over medium heat, heat the remaining olive oil. Pour in the egg mixture. Cook for 10 minutes, making sure to work the sides of the pan to prevent sticking.
7. Remove the pan from the heat. Place a plate face-down on top of the pan and flip. With the tortilla on the plate, return the pan to the stove and gently slide the tortilla back into the pan, cooked side up.
8. Cook for another 5 minutes, or until a toothpick poked in the center of the tortilla comes out clean. Remove from the heat.
9. Let cool for 10 minutes before slicing and serving.

Once Upon a Pesto

Some believe Spanish tortillas came about during wartime when a poor woman put together the only ingredients she had on hand—eggs, potatoes, and onion—for an army general when he visited her home.

Just Right

Spanish tortillas and frittatas can be very similar, but the dishes are finished differently. Frittatas are finished in the oven, and Spanish tortillas are cooked completely on the stovetop.

ONCE UPON A PESTO

CHAPTER 12: FRANCE
Broccoli Pesto
INSPIRED BY FRANCE

FOLK or FAIRY — NUT-FREE, SAVORY

MAKES 2 CUPS

TELLTALE and TIME — BEGINNER, 2 MINUTES

JESSICA PAHOLSKY

World War I GIs, whose initials stand for 'government issue' or 'general issue,' grew fond of eating broccoli during their service abroad. In 1919, the war officially ended with the signing of the Treaty of Versailles in a town near Paris, France. American soldiers then returned home from the war craving broccoli, and as a result, they created a demand for this green vegetable in the United States.

INGREDIENTS

- 2 cups cooked broccoli cuts
- 1/2 cup fresh tarragon
- 1 garlic clove, peeled
- 2 ounces Gouda cheese (or 1/3 cup cubed)
- 1/4 cup olive oil
- 1/2 teaspoon salt

DIRECTIONS

1. Combine all of the ingredients in a food processor. Blend until the desired consistency forms.

2. If using a mortar and pestle, mash the broccoli, tarragon, and garlic until smooth. Mix in the remaining ingredients. Mash until the desired consistency forms.

3. Store pesto in an airtight container or jar in the refrigerator for up to one week. Use throughout the week in the next two recipes. Pesto can last in an airtight container in the freezer for up to six months.

Once Upon a Pesto

Broccoli traces its roots to the Mediterranean, where it was created from a relative of cabbage. The word *broccoli* comes from an Italian noun that means 'the flowering crest of a cabbage.'

ONCE UPON A PESTO

Chicken Pot Pie Crêpes

MADE WITH BROCCOLI PESTO

MAKES 8 CRÊPES

TELLTALE *and* TIME

ADVANCED, 50 MINUTES

JESSICA PAHOLSKY

Chicken pot pie was a common ration for soldiers during World War I, a global war ended by a treaty signed in France. Several years prior in France, it's been said that a woman accidentally dribbled a thin porridge mixture onto a hot cooking surface. Thus, the *crêpe* was born.

INGREDIENTS

For the chicken pot pie filling:
1/4 cup peeled and chopped shallot
2 tablespoons butter
1 cup milk
2 tablespoons flour
1/2 cup Broccoli Pesto
1 cup cooked and cut broccoli
1 cup cooked and cut baby carrots
1 cup thawed frozen peas
1 cup cooked and sliced mushrooms
2 cups cooked and cut chicken breast

For the crêpe:
1 cup flour
2 eggs
1/2 cup milk
1/2 cup water
1/4 teaspoon salt
2 tablespoons melted butter
1 tablespoon olive oil

DIRECTIONS

1. In a large pan over medium-high heat, combine the shallot and butter. Cook until the shallot becomes transparent, about 3 minutes.
2. Add the milk, flour, and Broccoli Pesto. Stir for 3 minutes.
3. Add the remaining chicken pot pie filling ingredients and stir to incorporate. Reduce the heat, cover, and cook for 10 minutes.
4. Meanwhile, in a medium mixing bowl, combine the flour, eggs, milk, water, salt, and melted butter. Stir until smooth.
5. In a medium pan over medium-high heat, heat the oil. Scoop 1/4 cup of the crêpe batter into the hot pan. Tilt the pan to coat the pan with the batter, forming a thin circle.
6. Cook the crêpe until it turns golden brown, about 2 minutes. Flip the crêpe and cook for 2 more minutes.
7. Transfer the cooked crêpe to a serving plate.
8. Repeat steps 5 through 7 until all of the crêpe batter is used.
9. On each crêpe, scoop 1/3 cup of the chicken pot pie filling onto one quarter of the circle. Fold the empty half over the mixture, creating a half circle. Then fold in the resulting empty half of the half circle to form a quarter circle.
10. Repeat step 9 until all of the crêpes have been filled, and then serve.

Once Upon a Pesto

The word *crêpe* comes from the Old French word *crespe*, which is derived from the Latin word that means 'curled.' As *crêpes* cook, their edges ruffle, or curl, slightly.

Just Right

If you really want to be French, make this recipe on February 2, which is recognized as the day of *crêpes* in France.

French Toast BLT

MADE WITH BROCCOLI PESTO

MAKES 4 SANDWICHES

TELLTALE and TIME

INTERMEDIATE, 35 MINUTES

Once Upon a Pesto

The name French toast may have been first used in England during the 17th century. English settlers then brought the recipe to America.

JESSICA PAHOLSKY

Despite its name, French toast originated in Rome, not France, during the 4th century as a way to use up stale bread. In France, French toast is called *pain perdu*, or 'lost bread.' The process of soaking stale bread in a milk-egg mixture and then toasting it in a pan hasn't changed much throughout history.

INGREDIENTS

For the pesto mayo:
1 egg
1/2 teaspoon Dijon mustard
1/2 teaspoon salt
1 teaspoon fresh lemon juice
1 cup olive oil
1/3 cup Broccoli Pesto

For the French toast:
4 eggs
2/3 cup milk
2 tablespoons flour
2 teaspoons parsley flakes
salt and pepper to taste
8 slices of Texas toast bread
2 tablespoons butte

For the BLT:
1/2 head iceberg lettuce, leaves separated
8 slices cooked bacon
1 large tomato, sliced

DIRECTIONS

1. To make the mayo, combine the egg and Dijon in a blender. Blend for 1 minute.
2. Add the salt and lemon juice. Blend for another 30 seconds.
3. Add 1/4 cup olive oil at a time, blending for 10 seconds after each addition until all of the olive oil has been added. Transfer the mayo to a small dish.
4. Stir in the Broccoli Pesto into the mayo mixture until fully incorporated. Place the pesto mayo in the refrigerator to chill.
5. In a large mixing bowl, whisk together the eggs, milk, flour, parsley, salt, and pepper.
6. Soak each bread slice in the batter, flipping to coat both sides completely.
7. In a medium pan over medium heat, melt the butter. Transfer the soaked bread slices to the pan, one or two at a time.
8. Cook each slice for 3 minutes, or until golden brown. Flip each slice and cook for an additional 3 minutes.
9. Remove the cooked slices and set them on the cooling rack until all of the slices have been cooked.
10. Plate 4 slices of French toast on 4 plates. Then, layer on each the lettuce, bacon, and tomato.
11. On the remaining 4 slices of French toast, spread the pesto mayo. Place these slices mayo side down on top of the plated French toast slices and serve.

Thin bread does not work well for French toast. Choose bread that's sliced about 3/4 to 1 inch thick.

ONCE UPON A PESTO

CHAPTER 13: BELGIUM
Endive Pesto

INSPIRED BY BELGIUM

FOLK *or* FAIRY — SAVORY

MAKES 1 1/4 CUPS

TELLTALE *and* TIME — BEGINNER — 2 MINUTES

JESSICA PAHOLSKY

Endive is a younger addition to the vegetable family. In 1830, a farmer in Brussels, Belgium created it by accident. He was storing chicory roots in his cellar because his plan was to dry and roast them to make coffee. But, he left for several months to serve in war and returned to find endive sprouting in his cellar. This new member of the chicory family hit grocery store shelves 16 years later. Now, it's grown worldwide.

INGREDIENTS

1/4 cup shelled chopped walnuts

1 1/2 cups chopped endive

1 cup chopped D'Anjou pear (or 1/2 pear)

1/3 cup crumbled Roquefort cheese

1 tablespoon fresh thyme

1 tablespoon olive oil

DIRECTIONS

1. Combine all of the ingredients in a food processor. Blend until the desired consistency forms.

2. If using a mortar and pestle, crush the walnuts until a fine crumb forms. Add the endive and pear, and mash until smooth. Mix in the remaining ingredients. Mash until the desired consistency forms.

3. Store pesto in an airtight container or jar in the refrigerator for up to one week. Use throughout the week in the next two recipes. Pesto can last in an airtight container in the freezer for up to six months.

Once Upon a Pesto

The ironic part about the creation of endive is that this young vegetable grew from chicory, one of the earliest plants mentioned in recorded literature. Does that mean endive isn't really that new?

ONCE UPON A PESTO

Beet Brownies

MADE WITH ENDIVE PESTO

MAKES 12 SERVINGS

TELLTALE *and* TIME

INTERMEDIATE, 1 HOUR

JESSICA PAHOLSKY

Throughout Belgium, there are more than 2,000 chocolate shops. What sets Belgian chocolate apart from others is a high cocoa content. Belgium is also a place where sugar beet crops thrive. These root vegetables are used to produce beet sugar, a less processed variety of sugar.

INGREDIENTS

1/2 cup chopped cooked beets (or 1 large beet)

1 15-ounce can black beans, drained and rinsed

1 egg

1/2 cup brown sugar

1/4 cup cocoa powder

1/2 cup Endive Pesto

1 teaspoon baking powder

DIRECTIONS

1. Heat oven to 350° F.

2. Blend together the beets, black beans, and egg in a food processor until smooth.

3. Transfer the beet mixture to a medium-sized mixing bowl. Add the remaining ingredients and mix until incorporated.

4. Pour the brownie mixture into a lightly greased 8-by-8-inch baking pan. Wiggle the pan to evenly distribute the batter.

5. Bake for 30 minutes.

6. Let cool for at least 15 minutes before cutting the brownies.

7. Serve fresh, or store in an airtight container in the refrigerator for up to one week.

Once Upon a Pesto

It's said brownies were an accidental creation, much like endive's conception. A woman was baking a chocolate cake, but she didn't add the correct amount of baking powder or flour. This resulted in a denser version of the cake she meant to make, now called brownies.

Just Right

If you prefer a more firm brownie, let the brownies bake and cool completely to room temperature. Then, place the pan in the fridge for an hour or two before cutting them.

ONCE UPON A PESTO

Brussels Sprouts Gratin

MADE WITH ENDIVE PESTO

MAKES 4 TO 8 SERVINGS

TELLTALE *and* TIME

INTERMEDIATE, 1 HOUR

JESSICA PAHOLSKY

Although Brussels sprouts were first grown elsewhere, they were named during the 16th century when these mini cabbages were being harvested in Brussels, Belgium. A couple centuries later, French settlers brought Brussels sprouts to the United States.

INGREDIENTS

4 cups halved Brussels sprouts

1 cup grated Gruyère cheese (or 4 ounces)

2 tablespoons butter

3 tablespoons all-purpose flour

1 cup milk

2 garlic cloves, minced

1 cup Endive Pesto

1/4 cup Roquefort cheese

DIRECTIONS

1. Heat oven to 350° F.
2. Bring a large pot of water to a boil over high heat.
3. Boil the Brussels sprouts for 6 minutes, then transfer to a colander and rinse under cold running water.
4. Transfer the cooked Brussels sprouts to an 8-by-8-inch baking dish. Top with 1/2 cup grated Gruyère cheese. Set aside.
5. In a small saucepan over medium-low heat, melt the butter.
6. Add the flour to the saucepan and stir for 30 seconds.
7. Whisk in the milk, and then add the garlic and Endive Pesto. Cook for 2 minutes.
8. Pour the sauce over the Brussels sprouts. Top with the remaining Gruyère cheese and the Roquefort cheese.
9. Bake for 30 minutes, or until the cheese bubbles and starts to turn golden brown.
10. Let cool for 5 minutes before serving.

Once Upon a Pesto

The forerunner of Brussels sprouts dates back as far as ancient Rome.

Just Right

Using larger Brussels sprouts creates a strongerr cabbage taste. Smaller Brussels sprouts are sweeter. Understanding this difference can help you achieve the taste you prefer.

CHAPTER 14: SWEDEN
Rutabaga Pesto
INSPIRED BY SWEDEN

FOLK or FAIRY — NUT-FREE, DAIRY-FREE, SAVORY

MAKES 2 CUPS

TELLTALE and TIME — BEGINNER, 2 MINUTES

JESSICA PAHOLSKY

Rutabaga comes from a Swedish dialect and means 'short root.' A cross between turnip and cabbage, this root vegetable is commonly called swede because it was first raised during the late Middle Ages in Sweden, where citizens are also referred to as swedes.

INGREDIENTS

2 cups cubed rutabaga, cooked in 1 tablespoon olive oil for 15 minutes

1 medium golden delicious apple, chopped

2 tablespoons fresh rosemary

1 1/2 tablespoons fresh lemon juice

1/2 teaspoon ground cinnamon

1/4 cup water

DIRECTIONS

1. Combine all of the ingredients in a food processor. Blend until the desired consistency forms.

2. If using a mortar and pestle, mash the rutabaga, apple, and rosemary until smooth. Mix in the remaining ingredients. Mash until the desired consistency forms.

3. Store pesto in an airtight container or jar in the refrigerator for up to one week. Use throughout the week in the next two recipes. Pesto can last in an airtight container in the freezer for up to six months.

Once Upon a Pesto

Another name for rutabaga is Swedish turnip, indicating not only the root's origin, but also that Swedish people are some of the only frequent consumers of rutabaga.

ONCE UPON A PESTO

Sweet Buns

MADE WITH RUTABAGA PESTO

MAKES 12 SERVINGS

TELLTALE *and* TIME — ADVANCED — 2 HOURS AND 30 MINUTES

Once Upon a Pesto

Another popular place where you'll find *kanelbullar* is at coffee parties in Sweden. From sweet breads and cookies to pastries and cakes, this tradition highlights the role home baking plays in Swedish culture.

JESSICA PAHOLSKY

Kanelbullar, a popular bakery item in Sweden, are cinnamon buns made with cardamom dough, orange flavoring, and crunchy sugar. Sweet buns aren't usually overly sweet despite their English name.

INGREDIENTS

1 cup milk, lukewarm

2 1/4 teaspoons active dry yeast

1/3 cup sugar

3 1/2 cups all-purpose flour

1/2 teaspoon salt

1 egg

5 tablespoons unsalted butter, at room temperature

For the filling:

6 tablespoons unsalted butter, at room temperature

2 tablespoons sugar

6 tablespoons Rutabaga Pesto

For the egg wash:

1 egg whisked with 1 tablespoon water

Just Right

Celebrate National *Kanelbullar* Day, a Swedish tradition that began in 1999, on October 4 with this sweet buns recipe.

DIRECTIONS

1. To make the dough, in a small bowl, combine the milk, yeast, and 1 tablespoon sugar. Let sit for 15 minutes, or until foamy.
2. In a separate large mixing bowl, mix together the remaining sugar, flour, and salt. Add the egg.
3. Pour the milk and yeast mixture into the large mixing bowl. Mix until incorporated.
4. Add the butter and continue mixing until a smooth batter forms.
5. Cover the bowl with a damp towel or cling wrap, and leave in a warm area for 45 minutes, or until the dough has doubled in size.
6. Prepare the filling by combining all of the filling ingredients in a small mixing bowl. Mix until incorporated. Set aside.
7. Transfer the dough to a lightly floured surface. Roll the dough into a 24-by-15-inch rectangle.
8. Spread the filling evenly across the surface of the dough.
9. Working from one of the short edges, fold one third of the dough in toward the center, and repeat with the other short edge (folding the dough in thirds like a letter).
10. Transfer the folded dough to a cookie sheet and refrigerate for 15 minutes.
11. Place the folded dough onto a cutting board and cut with a pastry wheel into strips 3/4 inch wide.
12. Take each strip and twist it a couple of times before gently tying into a knot. Place the knotted bun onto a cookie sheet lined with parchment paper. Repeat this process until the folded dough has all been used. Be sure to leave 2 inches of space between each dough knot and the edges of the cookie sheet.
13. Cover the cookie sheet with cling wrap and let the dough knots rise in a warm area for 30 minutes.
14. Heat oven to 400° F.
15. Brush the dough knots with the egg wash.
16. Bake for 15 minutes, or until the edges begin to turn golden brown.
17. Let cool for 5 minutes, and then transfer to a wire cooling rack to cool for another 5 minutes.
18. Serve warm, or let cool completely before storing in an airtight container in the refrigerator for up to one week.

ONCE UPON A PESTO

Swedish Tuna Balls

MADE WITH RUTABAGA PESTO

MAKES 12 MEATBALLS

TELLTALE *and* TIME

INTERMEDIATE, 50 MINUTES

JESSICA PAHOLSKY

Smörgåsbord is a Swedish culinary tradition that usually includes Swedish meatballs, or *köttbullar*. These meatballs are made with ground meat and herbs, but swedes also eat fish balls called *fiskbullar*. With a coastline about 2,000 miles long, fish and preserving fish are traditional parts of Swedish culture.

INGREDIENTS

5 6-ounce cans tuna in water, drained

2 tablespoons plain breadcrumbs

2 tablespoons rolled oats

1/4 cup Rutabaga Pesto

For the gravy:

3 tablespoons butter

3 tablespoons flour

1 cup vegetable broth

salt and pepper to taste

DIRECTIONS

1. Heat oven to 350° F.
2. In a large mixing bowl, combine the tuna, breadcrumbs, oats, and Rutabaga Pesto. Mix together until incorporated, breaking the tuna apart with your fingers as you go.
3. Line a cookie sheet with lightly greased aluminum foil.
4. Divide the tuna mixture into 12 portions. Roll each portion into a ball, and then transfer to the prepared cookie sheet.
5. Bake for 20 to 25 minutes, flipping halfway.
6. To prepare the gravy, in a large pan over medium-low heat, melt the butter.
7. Whisk in the flour and then the broth. Add salt and pepper to taste.
8. Cook for 1 to 2 minutes, stirring constantly.
9. Once the tuna meatballs are done baking, add them to the pan and reduce the heat to a simmer.
10. Gently toss the meatballs in the gravy to coat while cooking for 5 minutes more.
11. Serve over mashed potatoes or egg noodles.

Once Upon a Pesto

Swedish meatballs are actually from Turkey. This signature Swedish dish was brought to Scandinavia by King Charles XII, who was living in exile in the Ottoman Empire during the early 18th century.

Just Right

If you have salmon on hand, you can use 1 3/4 pounds of already cooked salmon instead of tuna.

ONCE UPON A PESTO

CHAPTER 15: SWITZERLAND
Swiss Chard Pesto

INSPIRED BY SWITZERLAND

FOLK or FAIRY — SAVORY

MAKES 2 CUPS

TELLTALE and TIME — BEGINNER — 2 MINUTES

JESSICA PAHOLSKY

Chard comes from a Latin word that means 'artichoke thistle.' Furthermore, Swiss chard is not actually native to Switzerland. Instead, this leafy green comes from the Mediterranean. Swiss chard is a much older close relative of beets.

INGREDIENTS

1/3 cup shelled walnuts

15-20 leaves of Swiss chard, chopped

3 garlic cloves, peeled

1/2 cup Gruyère cheese, shaved

1 teaspoon salt

1/4 cup olive oil

1/4 cup apple cider vinegar

DIRECTIONS

1. Combine all of the ingredients in a food processor. Blend until the desired consistency forms.

2. If using a mortar and pestle, mash the broccoli, tarragon, and garlic until smooth. Mix in the remaining ingredients. Mash until the desired consistency forms.

3. Store pesto in an airtight container or jar in the refrigerator for up to one week. Use throughout the week in the next two recipes. Pesto can last in an airtight container in the freezer for up to six months.

Once Upon a Pesto

During the 19th century, a Swiss botanist determined the scientific name for Swiss chard. To honor his nationality, the leafy green earned its common name.

Leek Galette

MADE WITH SWISS CHARD PESTO

MAKES 12 SERVINGS

TELLTALE *and* TIME
ADVANCED, 2 HOURS

JESSICA PAHOLSKY

A landlocked nation, Switzerland is bordered by France, Italy, Germany, and Austria. Swiss cuisine is therefore largely influenced by these four neighbors. One French culinary influence is the *galette*, a flat puff pastry tart.

INGREDIENTS

For the crust:

2 cups flour
1 teaspoon salt
3/4 cup butter, chilled and cut into 1-inch cubes
1 tablespoon apple cider vinegar
1/4 cup cold water
1 egg, beaten (for the egg wash)

For the filling:

3 tablespoons olive oil
4 small Yukon gold potatoes, sliced 1/2 inch thick
1 leek, sliced 1/2 inch thick
3/4 cup ricotta cheese
1/2 cup Swiss Chard Pesto
1/4 cup Gruyère cheese, shaved
salt and pepper to taste

DIRECTIONS

1. Heat oven to 350°.
2. In a medium mixing bowl, combine the flour and salt. Cut in the butter.
3. Add the apple cider vinegar and water, and work until a smooth dough forms. Cover and place in the refrigerator.
4. In a large saucepan over medium-high heat, add the olive oil, potatoes, and leek. Cook for about 15 minutes, flipping every 5 minutes. Set aside.
5. Remove the dough from the refrigerator and form it into a ball.
6. On a greased counter, roll the dough into a circular crust about 1/8 inch thick.
7. Line a cookie sheet with parchment paper, and transfer the crust to the cookie sheet.
8. In a small mixing bowl, combine the ricotta and Swiss Chard Pesto. Spread the ricotta mixture over the crust, leaving the outermost 2 inches uncovered.
9. Arrange the potatoes and leeks atop the ricotta mixture. Place the Gruyère cheese on top. Add salt and pepper to taste.
10. Fold in the edges of the crust, creasing at the point where the ricotta mixture ends.
11. Brush the egg wash on the exposed crust.
12. Bake for 45 minutes, or until the crust is golden brown.
13. Let cool for 10 minutes before slicing and serving.

Once Upon a Pesto

The word *galette* comes from a Norman word that means 'flat cake.' *Galette* is considered a catch-all term for a free-form pastry base that's topped with sweet or savory ingredients.

Just Right

The thickness of the crust is important. Too thick, and it will be chewy. Too thin, and it won't serve its purpose well. Aim for a thickness of 1/8 inch.

Barley Minestrone

MADE WITH SWISS CHARD PESTO

MAKES 8 SERVINGS

TELLTALE and TIME

INTERMEDIATE, 1 HOUR

JESSICA PAHOLSKY

One of Switzerland's four neighbors is Italy. *Minestrone*, a popular Italian soup, comes from an Italian verb that means 'to dish up.' Thus, its recipe isn't written in stone. *Minestrone*'s ingredients vary from cook to cook and day to day.

INGREDIENTS

1 cup celery, chopped
1 cup red cabbage, sliced
1 cup carrot, chopped
1 cup onion, chopped
3 cups mushroom, sliced
2 tablespoons olive oil
salt to taste
1 cup pearled barley
1/2 cup Swiss Chard Pesto
2 cups vegetable stock
4 cups water

DIRECTIONS

1. In a large pot over medium-high heat, add the celery, cabbage, carrot, onion, mushroom, olive oil, and salt. Sauté for 10 minutes, stirring occasionally.

2. Reduce the heat to low. Add the barley, Swiss Chard Pesto, vegetable stock, and water. Cover and let simmer for 45 minutes.

3. Ladle the soup into serving bowls.

Once Upon a Pesto

Well before modern-day Italy, *minestrone* was eaten in what eventually came to be known as the Roman Empire. Even then, the ingredients were more or less similar to those of the current soup.

Just Right

Serve *minestrone* with crusty bread for a real comforting classic. If you are feeling extra cozy, add some Parmigiano Reggiano cheese shavings to your bowl of soup.

ONCE UPON A PESTO

CHAPTER 16: ITALY
Zucchini Pesto
INSPIRED BY ITALY

FOLK or FAIRY — SAVORY

MAKES 2 CUPS

TELLTALE and TIME — BEGINNER — 2 MINUTES

Jessica Paholsky

Zucchini and tomato are some of the most often used ingredients in Italian cooking. Zucchini is an Italian word meaning 'small squash.' That translation is pretty straightforward. However, the translation for tomato is a bit different. The Italian word for 'tomato'—*pomodoro*—literally means 'apple of gold.' This is because the first tomatoes known to Europeans were actually yellow, not red.

INGREDIENTS

2 tablespoons pine nuts

1 medium zucchini, chopped

1/3 cup sun-dried tomato halves

2 garlic cloves, peeled

1/3 cup grated Parmesan cheese

1/4 cup olive oil

1 teaspoon salt

DIRECTIONS

1. Combine all of the ingredients in a food processor. Blend until the desired consistency forms.

2. If using a mortar and pestle, crush the pine nuts until a fine crumb forms. Add the zucchini, sun-dried tomato, and garlic, and mash until smooth. Mix in the remaining ingredients. Mash until the desired consistency forms.

3. Store pesto in an airtight container or jar in the refrigerator for up to one week. Use throughout the week in the next two recipes. Pesto can last in an airtight container in the freezer for up to six months.

Once Upon a Pesto

The word *zucchini* is a plural diminutive of *zucca*, or 'one squash.' The diminutive form of *zucca* is *zucchino*.

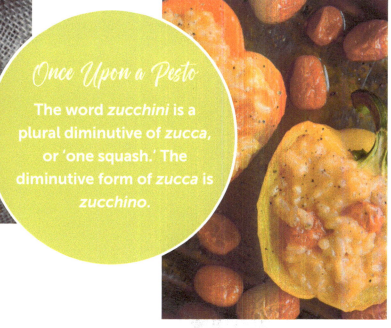

ONCE UPON A PESTO

Risotto-Stuffed Peppers

MADE WITH ZUCCHINI PESTO

MAKES 6 SERVINGS

TELLTALE *and* TIME
INTERMEDIATE, 1 HOUR AND 15 MINUTES

Once Upon a Pesto
Since *risotto* was created in the northern Italian city, Milan, the dish's full name is *risotto alla Milanese*.

JESSICA PAHOLSKY

Risotto is the most common use of rice in Italy. It's particularly popular among northern Italians. Rice first arrived in Sicily during the Middle Ages. Over time, the rice that grew best in Italy's climate was a short-grain variety. Arborio rice is also a short grain, and it's used to make *risotto*, a creamy *primo*, or 'first-course dish.'

INGREDIENTS

1 pint grape tomatoes

1 teaspoon salt

6 tablespoons olive oil

3 bell peppers, halved lengthwise

1/2 cup diced onion

4 cups vegetable broth

1 cup Arborio rice

1 cup dry white wine

1/2 cup Zucchini Pesto

DIRECTIONS

1. Heat oven to 400° F.
2. In a small baking pan, toss the tomatoes in salt and 2 tablespoons of olive oil.
3. In a medium baking pan, brush the bell pepper halves with 1 tablespoon of olive oil. Transfer the bell peppers to a large baking pan.
4. Bake the tomatoes and the bell peppers for 25 minutes. Set aside when done.
5. While the vegetables roast in the oven, combine the remaining 3 tablespoons of olive oil and the onion in a large pan over medium heat. Stir continuously for 5 minutes, or until onions become translucent.
6. Add the rice to the onion mixture. Stir to coat the rice, and then cook for 2 minutes.
7. Add the white wine to the rice. Stir continuously until the wine cooks off, about 5 minutes.
8. Meanwhile, in a small pot, bring the vegetable broth to a simmer.
9. Add one ladle of the simmering broth to the rice. Stir continuously until the rice has absorbed most of the broth. Repeat until one ladle is left.
10. Add the final ladle of broth and the Zucchini Pesto to the rice. Stir until mostly absorbed, but still a little runny. Remove from the heat.
11. Add the roasted tomatoes to the risotto and gently fold in.
12. Scoop the risotto into the bell pepper halves and serve.

Just Right

One of the ingredients often used in Italy when making *risotto* is a spice called saffron. If you wish to follow suit, in step 7, when adding the white wine to the rice, also add a pinch of saffron.

ONCE UPON A PESTO

Eggplant Parmesan Lasagna Stacks

MADE WITH ZUCCHINI PESTO

MAKES 8 SERVINGS

TELLTALE *and* TIME

INTERMEDIATE, 1 HOUR

Once Upon a Pesto

It's often assumed that eggplant Parmesan came from Parma, the city in northern Italy, or is named after the cheese, Parmigiano Reggiano. All three sound and are spelled similarly.

JESSICA PAHOLSKY

In Italy, eggplant Parmesan is called *parmigiana di melanzane.* The dish's name comes from the Sicilian word *parmiciana,* which means 'shutters.' On the other hand, *lasagna* is not originally from Italy. This now Italian classic was first made in ancient Greece.

INGREDIENTS

1 cup flour

2 eggs, whisked

1 1/2 cups panko bread crumbs

1 tablespoon dried basil

2 teaspoons salt

1 medium eggplant, cut into 15 slices about 1/2 inch thick

1/4 cup olive oil

1 cup ricotta cheese

1 cup Zucchini Pesto

1 cup tomato sauce

1/2 cup shredded mozzarella cheese

DIRECTIONS

1. Heat oven to 375° F.
2. Prepare three small bowls: the first with flour; the second with eggs; and the third with panko bread crumbs, basil, and salt mixed together.
3. Coat each eggplant slice with the flour first, the egg second, and the bread crumb mixture third.
4. In a large pan over medium-high heat, add the olive oil. Heat until water sizzles when dropped in.
5. Place as many of the coated eggplant slices as you can fit in a single layer in the pan. Fry until golden brown, about 2 minutes each side.
6. Transfer the fried eggplant to a paper towel-lined plate. Repeat step 4 until all eggplant slices are fried.
7. Meanwhile, mix the ricotta cheese and Zucchini Pesto in a small bowl.
8. Grease a medium baking pan. Place 5 fried eggplant slices in a single layer in the pan, with an inch of space between each.
9. Spoon a heaping 1 tablespoon of the ricotta mixture on each fried eggplant slice, followed by 1 tablespoon of tomato sauce. Place another eggplant slice on each stack and gently press until the filling reaches the edge of the eggplant slice.
10. Repeat step 8 two more times so there are a total of three layers each of eggplant, ricotta mixture, and tomato sauce in each of the 5 stacks.
11. Top each stack with a pinch of mozzarella cheese.
12. Bake for 30 minutes, or until the mozzarella cheese has melted and begins turning golden brown.
13. Let cool for 5 minutes before serving.

Just Right

If you find eggplant to be bitter, one way to get rid of that taste is to sprinkle the eggplant slices with a little salt, and let them sit for 30 minutes. Then, rinse the salt off of the eggplant slices, and pat them dry before continuing with step 3.

ONCE UPON A PESTO

CHAPTER 17: CROATIA
Plum Pesto
INSPIRED BY CROATIA

FOLK or FAIRY
DAIRY-FREE, SWEET

MAKES 1 ¾ CUPS

TELLTALE and TIME
BEGINNER — 2 MINUTES

JESSICA PAHOLSKY

The world's largest producers of plum are the countries of former Yugoslavia, including Croatia. In fact, several traditional Croatian recipes incorporate this stone fruit. Some examples include meat stews, plum and cheese dumplings, jam for pastries, and even spirits.

INGREDIENTS

1/2 cup shelled walnuts

3 medium-sized plums, quartered and seeded

1/2 teaspoon cardamom

1/8 teaspoon ground cloves

DIRECTIONS

1. Combine all of the ingredients in a food processor. Blend until the desired consistency forms.

2. If using a mortar and pestle, crush the walnuts until a fine crumb forms. Add the plums and mash until smooth. Mix in the remaining ingredients. Mash until the desired consistency forms.

3. Store pesto in an airtight container or jar in the refrigerator for up to one week. Use throughout the week in the next two recipes. Pesto can last in an airtight container in the freezer for up to six months.

Once Upon a Pesto

Plums have a long and interesting history. It's been said they were domesticated in China more than 2,000 years ago. In his writing, Confucius, the great Chinese philosopher, praised the fruit.

Stone Fruit Salsa

MADE WITH PLUM PESTO

MAKES 8 SERVINGS

TELLTALE *and* TIME

BEGINNER, 5 MINUTES

Jessica Paholsky

Nearly every city in Croatia has its own outdoor market, or *pazar*, where locals and tourists shop. In summertime, these local food hubs feature fruits like berries, apricots, peaches, plums, cherries, and melons.

INGREDIENTS

4 cups chopped mixed stone-fruit (peach, nectarine, cherry, apricot)

1/4 cup Plum Pesto

pinch of salt

DIRECTIONS

1. In a large mixing bowl, toss together all of the ingredients.
2. Store in an airtight container until ready to serve.

Once Upon a Pesto

Croatia's *pazar* is comparable to Turkey's *bazaar*, which is a word that means 'place of prices.'

Just Right

Beyond a dip for tortilla chips, salsa can also be used to top chicken, fish, or a salad.

Walnut Swirl Bread

MADE WITH PLUM PESTO

MAKES 8 SERVINGS

TELLTALE *and* TIME

ADVANCED, 3 HOURS AND 25 MINUTES

Once Upon a Pesto

Relatives of Croatian *povitica* are Slovenian *potica* and Russian *babka*. All three are yeast breads featuring layers or swirls of some kind of filling.

JESSICA PAHOLSKY

In Croatia, *povitica* is a dessert common during Christmas and Easter. It's a sweet bread made with pastry dough that's rolled out very thin, coated with a groundnut paste, and then folded into a loaf pan. Its name comes from the Slovenian word that means 'to wrap in.'

INGREDIENTS

For the bread dough:

3 tablespoons sugar, plus 2 pinches for sprinkling

1 1/2 teaspoons active dry yeast

1/2 cup milk

3/4 teaspoon salt

2 eggs

2 tablespoons unsalted butter, melted

2 teaspoons vanilla

2 1/2 cups all-purpose flour

For the filling:

1 1/2 cups shelled ground walnuts

1/4 cup sugar

1 egg

1/4 teaspoon salt

Just Right

Eating *povitica* is plain and simple, but other ways to enjoy this dessert bread include heating it on a griddle or warming up a buttered slice in the microwave.

DIRECTIONS

1. To make the dough: In a large mixing bowl, dissolve the sugar in 2 tablespoons of warm water. Stir in the yeast and let stand for 10 minutes.
2. In a small saucepan over medium heat, bring the milk to a simmer. Add the salt and whisk together. Then, add the warm milk mixture to the yeast mixture.
3. Add the eggs, 1 tablespoon of butter, and vanilla to the yeast mixture. Stir to incorporate.
4. Gradually stir the flour into the yeast mixture. Mix until a dough forms.
5. On a floured surface, knead the dough for 5 minutes, adding flour to prevent sticking.
6. Place the dough in a lightly greased bowl. Cover and let rise until doubled in size, about 2 hours.
7. Meanwhile, prepare the filling by mixing together the walnuts and sugar. Add the egg and mix until incorporated. Stir in the salt and Plum Pesto, mixing until smooth. Set aside.
8. Heat oven to 350° F.
9. Grease a loaf pan. Divide the dough in half. Roll each dough half into a 16-by-10-inch rectangle.
10. Brush half of the filling mixture onto one dough half, leaving a 1/2-inch border along one of the long edges uncovered. Starting with the long edge opposite of the uncovered edge, roll the dough into a cylinder. Cut the cylinder in half.
11. Place halves side by side in a loaf pan.
12. Repeat step 9 with the other dough half and the rest of the filling mixture. Place these two half cylinders on top of the first two in the loaf pan.
13. Cover and let rise for 1 hour more.
14. Brush the top surface of the dough with 1 tablespoon of melted butter and sprinkle lightly with sugar.
15. Bake for 45 minutes, or until the crust turns golden brown.
16. Let cool in the pan for 10 minutes. Transfer the bread to a wire rack to cool completely before slicing and serving.

ONCE UPON A PESTO

CHAPTER 18: GREECE

Parsley Pesto

INSPIRED BY GREECE

FOLK *or* FAIRY: DAIRY-FREE, SAVORY

MAKES 1/2 CUPS

TELLTALE *and* TIME: BEGINNER, 2 MINUTES

JESSICA PAHOLSKY

For competitors in Greek athletic games, which can be equated to modern-day Olympics, the material goal was not a gold medal. Instead, the winners received a crown of parsley. At the time, this herb was not viewed as a food because ancient Greeks held parsley sacred.

INGREDIENTS

1/4 cup shelled walnuts

2 loosely-packed cups fresh parsley

2 loosely-packed cups fresh dill

2 garlic cloves

1/2 teaspoon ground cumin

1/4 cup olive oil

DIRECTIONS

1. Combine all of the ingredients in a food processor. Blend until the desired consistency forms.

2. If using a mortar and pestle, crush the walnuts until a fine crumb forms. Add the parsley, dill, and garlic, and mash until smooth. Mix in the remaining ingredients. Mash until the desired consistency forms.

3. Store pesto in an airtight container or jar in the refrigerator for up to one week. Use throughout the week in the next two recipes. Pesto can last in an airtight container in the freezer for up to six months.

Once Upon a Pesto

Ancient Greeks viewed parsley as sacred because according to ancient Greek legend, the plant grew out of the blood of hero Archemorus when he was killed and eaten by serpents.

ONCE UPON A PESTO

Dolmades

MADE WITH PARSLEY PESTO

MAKES 4 TO 8 SERVINGS

TELLTALE *and* TIME

INTERMEDIATE, 1 HOUR

Jessica Paholsky

Dolmades are one of the most iconic dishes in Greek cuisine. But, these rice-stuffed grape leaves were first made in Turkey, where *dolma* is a word that means 'something filled.' The dish's other common cousin is stuffed peppers.

INGREDIENTS

1/3 cup olive oil

1/8 teaspoon salt

1/8 teaspoon pepper

3 tablespoons Parsley Pesto

1/2 cup uncooked rice

1 3/4 cup water

1/4 cup shelled chopped walnuts

20 grape leaves, rinsed with warm water and patted dry

DIRECTIONS

1. In a small pot over medium-low heat, combine the olive oil, salt, pepper, and Parsley Pesto. Stir to combine. Simmer for 2 minutes.
2. Add to the pot the uncooked rice and 3/4 cup water. Cook, stirring every 2 to 3 minutes, for 10 minutes or until most of the water is absorbed. Transfer the rice mixture to a bowl and let cool.
3. Once the rice mixture has cooled to room temperature, stir in the walnuts.
4. Prepare the grape leaves by laying 16 of the grape leaves smooth side down. Then cut off the stems.
5. Scoop 1 tablespoon of the rice mixture on a grape leaf just above the removed stem. Fold the bottom flaps of the grape leaf over the rice. Then roll the grape leaf toward the top point of the leaf for one rotation. Fold in both sides of the leaf, then roll to the top point of the leaf.
6. Repeat step 5 for each of the 16 prepared grape leaves.
7. In a large saucepan over medium-high heat, spread flat the remaining 4 grape leaves to cover the surface. Place each stuffed grape leaf seam side down in the pan. Pour the remaining 1 cup of water over the stuffed grape leaves. Place a heat-safe plate on top to prevent the grape leaves from unrolling.
8. Cook for 30 to 35 minutes.
9. Gently remove the stuffed grape leaves with a slotted spoon and transfer to a serving plate.
10. Serve warm, or allow to chill if serving cold.

Once Upon a Pesto

Dolmades are also popular in Iran, Armenia, Iraq, and Turkey. Each variation of the recipe is unique. Some use cabbage instead of grape leaves. The fillings also vary and can include vegetables, herbs and spices, meat, and rice.

Just Right

The length of cooking time for *dolmades* allows the flavor from the grape leaves to soak into the filling. The trick is to cook it long enough to allow for this, but not too long or else the leaves will burn.

Hummus Bowl

MADE WITH PARSLEY PESTO

MAKES 4 TO 6 SERVINGS

TELLTALE *and* TIME

INTERMEDIATE, 30 MINUTES

Once Upon a Pesto

Hummus has been made all over the world for centuries. Many cultures among Middle Eastern and Mediterranean countries claim *hummus* as their own dish.

JESSICA PAHOLSKY

Hummus, which is the Arabic word for 'chickpea,' and it traces its roots back to the 13th century in Egypt. After years and years of trade between Egypt and Greece, *hummus* arrived in Greece and is now a modern staple.

INGREDIENTS

For the pita chips:
1 piece pita bread
2 teaspoons olive oil
pinch of paprika
pinch of salt

For the hummus:
1 15.5-ounce can chickpeas
2 tablespoons Parsley Pesto
2 tablespoons olive oil
1 tablespoon lemon juice

For the vinaigrette:
juice of 1 tangerine
1 tablespoon lemon juice
1 tablespoon honey
1 tablespoon balsamic vinegar
2 tablespoons olive oil

1 10-ounce bag greens (mixed greens, spinach, etc.)
1 avocado, pitted, peeled, and sliced
1 bell pepper, seeded and chopped
1/4 red onion, peeled and sliced
1 small cucumber, sliced
2 tangerines, peeled and divided

Just Right

Double the *hummus* part of this recipe, and reserve half of it for later use. It's a great veggie dip replacement for ranch.

DIRECTIONS

1. Heat oven to 400° F.

2. Using a pizza cutter, slice the pita bread into 8 to 12 equal pieces.

3. Brush the pita bread pieces lightly with olive oil. Then sprinkle them with a pinch of paprika and a pinch of salt.

4. Transfer seasoned pita bread pieces to a cookie sheet.

5. Bake for 8 to 10 minutes, then remove. Let cool slightly before adding to the salads.

6. While the pita bread pieces are baking, in a food processor, combine the hummus ingredients. Pulse until the desired consistency is achieved, adding an additional 1 teaspoon of olive oil at a time if too thick. Set aside.

7. In a small bowl, whisk together the vinaigrette ingredients. Set aside.

8. Arrange on each serving plate the salad greens. Divide evenly among each plate of salad greens the avocado, bell pepper, red onion, cucumber, tangerine, and hummus.

9. Drizzle over each salad plate the vinaigrette.

10. Divide the baked pita chips among the salad plates.

ONCE UPON A PESTO

CHAPTER 19: CYPRUS
Caper Pesto
INSPIRED BY CYPRUS

FOLK *or* FAIRY — SAVORY

MAKES 1 CUP

TELLTALE *and* TIME — BEGINNER — 2 MINUTES

JESSICA PAHOLSKY

Capers are the edible flower buds of a bush that thrives in the hot and dry climate of Mediterranean countries like Cyprus. Their harvesting is laborious. One by one, capers are picked by hand due to their delicate nature. Next, capers are sorted by size and dried or brined.

INGREDIENTS

1/4 cup shelled almonds

3 cups baby arugula

3 tablespoons capers, plus 4 teaspoons liquid from jar

1/2 cup freshly grated Parmigiano Reggiano cheese

1 tablespoon fresh lemon juice

2 tablespoons extra virgin olive oil

DIRECTIONS

1. Combine all of the ingredients in a food processor. Blend until the desired consistency forms.

2. If using a mortar and pestle, crush the almonds until a fine crumb forms. Add the arugula and capers, and mash until smooth. Mix in the remaining ingredients. Mash until the desired consistency forms.

3. Store pesto in an airtight container or jar in the refrigerator for up to one week. Use throughout the week in the next two recipes. Pesto can last in an airtight container in the freezer for up to six months.

Once Upon a Pesto

Capers are a very old commodity. They likely originated in western and central Asia, and there's mention of them on clay tablets dating back to nearly 5,000 years ago.

Feta Dip

MADE WITH CAPER PESTO

MAKES 10 TO 12 SERVINGS

TELLTALE *and* TIME

BEGINNER, 5 MINUTES

JESSICA PAHOLSKY

On the island of Cyprus, *halloumi* is recognized as the national cheese. But, feta could be just as easily found and enjoyed, and it hails from neighboring Greece. Feta is a versatile cheese that can be used as a garnish or as the main ingredient, much like *halloumi.*

INGREDIENTS

1 1/2 cups crumbled feta cheese

1/4 cup cream cheese

1/2 cup sour cream

2 tablespoons Caper Pesto

DIRECTIONS

1. Heat oven to 350° F.
1. Combine all of the ingredients in a food processor. Blend until smooth.
2. Transfer the dip to a small bowl to serve.
3. Cover the bowl with cling wrap or transfer to an airtight container, and store in the fridge for one to two weeks.

Once Upon a Pesto

In addition to a shared cuisine, Cyprus and Greece have common heritages, language, and religions.

Just Right

Great dipping options include chopped fresh tomato, toasted pita bread triangles, and cucumber slices. Take it one step further, and use feta dip for dunking pieces of asparagus and zucchini.

ONCE UPON A PESTO

Sheftalia

MADE WITH CAPER PESTO

MAKES 4 TO 6 SERVINGS

TELLTALE *and* TIME

NTERMEDIATE, 25 MINUTES

Jessica Paholsky

In Cyprus, *sheftalia* is a barbecued street food. Its name comes from the Turkish word for 'kebab.' One theory claims the dish got its name from a street vendor who's credited for inventing this meat-based item.

INGREDIENTS

1 pound ground beef (you can also use veal, pork, lamb, or a mixture of meats)

1/4 cup Caper Pesto

1 egg

2 tablespoons chopped fresh parsley

1/4 teaspoon ground black pepper

4 to 6 metal skewers

DIRECTIONS

1. Heat oven to a broil.
2. In a large mixing bowl, combine the meat, Caper Pesto, egg, parsley, and pepper. Knead the meat mixture with your hands until all of the ingredients are fully incorporated.
3. Divide the meat mixture into 4 to 6 equal portions, depending on how many skewers and servings are desired.
4. Line a rimmed baking sheet with foil.
5. Roll one meat mixture portion into a log about 2 inches wide and 1 inch thick. Place a skewer on top of the log lengthwise, and wrap the sides of the meat up and around the skewer, pinching to seal.
6. Roll the meat to form a uniform thickness of about 1 1/2 inches.
7. Transfer the skewered meat to the baking sheet.
8. Repeat steps 4 through 6 with the remaining meat and skewers.
9. Broil for 5 minutes.
10. Remove from the oven, rotate the meat skewers, and broil for another 5 minutes.
11. Serve the meat skewers over salad greens or with a side of cooked rice.

Once Upon a Pesto

Sheftalia are traditionally made by wrapping lamb and pork meat in caul fat, instead of traditional sausage casing. Then, as the skewers cook over a fire, the fat drips and causes the flame to brush up onto the meat, creating a nice crust similar to the effects of broiling.

Just Right

Another method for preparing *sheftalia* is on a gas or electric grill. This produces a nice char on the exterior of the meat.

CHAPTER 20: GEORGIA
Grape Pesto
INSPIRED BY GEORGIA

FOLK *or* FAIRY — SWEET

MAKES 1¾ CUPS

TELLTALE *and* TIME — BEGINNER — 2 MINUTES

JESSICA PAHOLSKY

Georgia is a nation that straddles Europe and Asia. The country boasts over 450 grape varieties among its roughly 500 acres of vineyards. A significant number of Georgia's grapes are used in winemaking, a process that began there over 8,000 years ago.

INGREDIENTS

1/3 cup shelled walnuts

2 cups red seedless grapes, rinsed and pat dry

2 tablespoons fresh rosemary

2 oz goat cheese

2 tablespoons honey

1 tablespoon red wine vinegar

DIRECTIONS

1. Combine all of the ingredients in a food processor. Blend until the desired consistency forms.

2. If using a mortar and pestle, crush the walnuts until a fine crumb forms. Add the grapes and rosemary, and mash until smooth. Mix in the remaining ingredients. Mash until the desired consistency forms.

3. Store pesto in an airtight container or jar in the refrigerator for up to one week. Use throughout the week in the next two recipes. Pesto can last in an airtight container in the freezer for up to six months.

Once Upon a Pesto

In addition to accounting for almost 20 percent of the world's total grape varieties, Georgia also grows endangered vines that aren't grown anywhere else on the planet.

ONCE UPON A PESTO

Eggplant Rolls

MADE WITH GRAPE PESTO

MAKES 10 TO 12 SERVINGS

TELLTALE *and* TIME

INTERMEDIATE, 1 HOUR

JESSICA PAHOLSKY

Eggplant rolls are traditionally served at Georgian feasts, called *supras*. They're made of eggplant slices filled with a blend of garlic and walnuts. The dish is usually served with other vegetable starters.

INGREDIENTS

2 medium eggplants, ends removed and cut lengthwise into 1/4-inch-thick slices

salt

1/2 cup olive oil

1/2 cup shelled walnuts

3 garlic cloves, peeled

1/4 cup water

1/2 cup Grape Pesto

DIRECTIONS

1. Generously salt each side of the eggplant slices. Let sit for 30 minutes before rinsing with cool water and patting dry.
2. In a large pan over medium heat, warm the olive oil. Add the eggplant slices in a single layer.
3. Cook each eggplant slice until it turns golden brown, about 5 minutes on each side. Be sure not to let the eggplant overcook or blacken. This will make rolling harder.
4. Transfer the cooked eggplant slice to a paper towel-lined plate.
5. Repeat steps 3 through 5 until all of the eggplant slices are cooked. Then let cool.
6. To make the filling, in a food processor, blend the walnuts until a fine powder forms. Transfer to a bowl.
7. Next in the food processor, blend the garlic and 1/4 cup water until smooth.
8. Add the Grape Pesto and walnut powder to the food processor. Blend until thick and smooth.
9. Spoon 1 tablespoon of the filling onto the center of each eggplant slice. Roll the slice around the filling.
10. Repeat step 9 with each eggplant slice, and then serve.

Once Upon a Pesto

Hinted by these eggplant rolls, Georgian cuisine is simple yet bursting with rich flavors. Major food categories in the country's diet include meat, wine, fresh vegetables, nuts, cheeses, and local herbs and spices.

Just Right

A traditional Georgian *supra* involves a large table, a big occasion to celebrate, plenty of food, and wine for the toast.

Churchkhela

MADE WITH GRAPE PESTO

MAKES 10 TO 20 SERVINGS

TELLTALE *and* TIME

ADVANCED, 3 TO 4 DAYS

JESSICA PAHOLSKY

Sweets in Georgia are usually made with sugar, nuts, and fruit. *Churchkhela*, for example, is a traditional Georgian candy that traces its roots to the Caucasus region. The main ingredients are grape must, nuts, and flour.

INGREDIENTS

- String and a needle
- 100 shelled walnut halves
- 5 cups cranberry-pomegranate juice
- 1 cup Grape Pesto
- 3/4 cup sugar
- 1 cup flour

DIRECTIONS

1. Thread a needle with a piece of string that's at least one foot in length.
2. With a walnut half lying flat, thread the needle through top to bottom. Repeat with 10 walnut halves.
3. Knot each end of the string so that the walnuts are touching, but not too tight. Be sure to leave one end with excess thread for holding throughout the next steps.
4. Repeat steps 2 through 3 nine more times to make 10 strands total, each with 10 walnut halves.
5. In a large saucepan over medium heat, add the juice, Grape Pesto, and sugar. Cook for about 5 minutes, making sure not to boil.
6. In a medium bowl, add the flour.
7. Slowly pour half of the warm juice mixture into the bowl of flour, stirring with a whisk to prevent clumping.
8. Transfer the flour-juice mixture to the saucepan, continuing to whisk.
9. Reduce the heat to a simmer and cook, stirring constantly, for 15 minutes.
10. Dip each walnut strand into the juice in the saucepan, making sure to coat fully.
11. Hang the strand on a rod suspended over old newspaper pages to catch all of the drippings. Let stand for 20 minutes.
12. Repeat steps 10 through 11 three to five more times, keeping the juice mixture warm for each coating.
13. Let the completed strands hang to dry for 3 to 4 days.
14. Remove the strands from the rod, and slice into pieces before serving.

Once Upon a Pesto

***Churchkhela* is often a snack eaten between meals. In Georgia, people also serve this candy during Christmas and New Year celebrations.**

Just Right

Traditional *churchkhela* use any or all of the following: almonds, walnuts, hazelnuts, and chocolate. Experiment with these different nuts, or stick to the one you like most.

ONCE UPON A PESTO

PART 3: Asia

As the largest continent and with more than 40 countries, Asia could be considered the mecca of the culinary world. The food history in this part of the globe is just as vast, beginning tens of thousands of centuries ago in what is today Western Asia.

When digging into Asia's food history, archaeological findings paint a partial picture. There is evidence of different kinds of nuts and fruits found in caves in Northern Iraq as well as wild grains found in present-day Jordan. As the domestication of fruits, grains, and other foods expanded, animals were also on the list. During the 9th century BC, pigs were first domesticated in China. Centuries thereafter, new fruits and grains sprung up throughout Asia. Some examples include citron in India, pomegranate in Syria, as well as millet and rice in China.

Sauce Similarity in Asia

Like many fruits, vegetables, and herbs, there's a sauce with ancient roots in Asia. Over 2,000 years ago, *chutney* was developed in India using fresh ingredients. Fresh is the common denominator between *chutney* and pesto; it's all about using local and in-season ingredients. Most *chutneys* are made primarily of fruits and spices, but there is no specific combination of ingredients. From a condiment to a dipping sauce, the sauce is also diverse in its use.

The word *chutney* comes from a Hindi word and variant that means 'to lick' or 'to eat with appetite.' From India, the sauce and its method of preserving foods was adopted by the Romans, and then it spread to other European countries. Finally, *chutney* reached America and Australia.

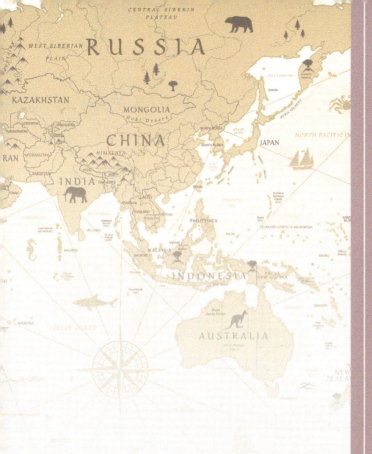

21. ARMENIA

22. IRAN

23. INDIA

24. RUSSIA

25. CHINA

26. KOREA

27. JAPAN

28. MALAYSIA

29. THAILAND

30. MYANMAR

Over time, as on other continents, certains foods, food combinations, and methods for preparing these foods took hold and rooted themselves in Asian cultures. There are a handful of commonalities that unify Asian cuisine as a whole. But, individually, each country touts a unique cuisine based on its local resources and the arrival of foreign foods. In fact, it wasn't until the 16th century that starches like corn and sweet potatoes traveled from the Americas to China via the Philippines. With a lengthier local history, rice is the staple starch throughout Asia, and it appears in many different varieties.

With rice as the base, Asian cuisines distinguish themselves through sauces and mixtures of spices. Ginger, for example, traces its origins to Asia. It's a common ingredient in curry, a popular dish in South Asia, Southeast Asia, and East Asia. East Asian cuisine is arguably most well known in other areas of the world. It includes Chinese, Japanese, Korean, and Taiwanese food. Some staple ingredients in these countries are noodles, soybeans, seafood, and tea. A close second to East Asian cuisine in terms of global popularity is South Asian cuisine, thanks to India's culinary contributions. Meanwhile, in West Asia, the food culture is more differentiated and less widespread beyond its borders. Common ingredients here are olives, honey, chickpeas, and parsley.

Just as important as ingredients, kitchen equipment in Asia also stands out as tried and true throughout the world. From the wok to bamboo steamers, cultures throughout Asia can claim many different cooking processes and dishes. The culinary tools that stand the test of time prove a tradition is both strong and delicious.

ONCE UPON A PESTO

CHAPTER 21: ARMENIA
Cantaloupe Pesto
INSPIRED BY ARMENIA

FOLK *or* FAIRY — DAIRY-FREE, SWEET

MAKES 1 1/2 CUPS

TELLTALE *and* TIME — BEGINNER, 2 MINUTES

JESSICA PAHOLSKY

During the 16th century, cantaloupe seeds made their way from Armenia to Cantalupo, a town near Italy's capital Rome. Cantaloupe was then named after that town. More recently, fruits like cantaloupe are common ingredients in Armenian kitchens.

INGREDIENTS

1/4 cup pine nuts

2 cups 1-inch cantaloupe pieces

1/4 cup fresh tarragon

1 tablespoon pomegranate juice

1/2 tablespoon fresh lemon juice

DIRECTIONS

1. Combine all of the ingredients in a food processor. Blend until the desired consistency forms.

2. If using a mortar and pestle, crush the pine nuts until a fine crumb forms. Add the cantaloupe and mash until smooth. Mix in the remaining ingredients. Mash until the desired consistency forms.

3. Store pesto in an airtight container or jar in the refrigerator for up to one week. Use throughout the week in the next two recipes. Pesto can last in an airtight container in the freezer for up to six months.

Once Upon a Pesto

While Italians are proud that their town Cantalupo inspired a fruit's name, it was the French who actually called the melon *cantaloup*, whose English version is cantaloupe.

ONCE UPON A PESTO

Fruit Leather

MADE WITH CANTALOUPE PESTO

MAKES 6 SERVINGS

TELLTALE *and* TIME

INTERMEDIATE, 4 HOURS

JESSICA PAHOLSKY

Nanny candy, which is also called *bastegh*, is a fruit leather found in Armenia. It's made with pureed fresh fruit, baked at a low temperature, and then cut and rolled. The process of making fruit leather at home began with Armenians and Persians when they realized they could preserve fruit this way.

INGREDIENTS

1 1/2 cups hulled and quartered strawberries

1/2 cup Cantaloupe Pesto

2 tablespoons sugar

DIRECTIONS

1. Heat oven to 175° F.
2. In a food processor, combine all of the ingredients. Blend until smooth.
3. Line a large rimmed baking tray with parchment paper. Pour the mixture over the parchment paper.
4. Using a spatula, spread the mixture into an even layer about 1/8 inch thick.
5. Bake for 3 hours and 30 minutes, or until tacky but not sticky. Let cool for 20 minutes.
6. Remove the fruit leather from the tray by lifting the parchment paper with the fruit leather atop. Place a sheet of wax paper on top of the fruit leather, and then flip it over so the wax paper is on the bottom.
7. Gently peel the parchment paper off of the fruit leather.
8. Slice the fruit leather into the desired width, and roll tightly.
9. Store in an air-tight container in the fridge for up to one month.

Once Upon a Pesto

While grocery stores carry fruit leather in snack-size rolls, *bastegh* is traditionally made in sheets nearly the size of a small blanket or towel.

Just Right

If you have a dehydrator, you can use this appliance's trays instead in step 3. And when you reach step 5, instead of baking, dry the mixture in your dehydrator at 145° F for 6 to 8 hours.

Orzo Pilaf

MADE WITH CANTALOUPE PESTO

MAKES 4 TO 6 SERVINGS

TELLTALE *and* TIME

BEGINNER, 10 MINUTES

144

JESSICA PAHOLSKY

Pilaf is an Armenian staple. It's an easy-to-prepare, grain-based dish that's flavored with meat, vegetables, or fruits. Rice and bulgar are typical grains used as the base in this dish.

INGREDIENTS

8 ounces orzo, cooked according to package directions and then drained and chilled

1 15-ounce can chickpeas, rinsed and drained

1 cup chopped cucumber

1/2 cup crumbled feta cheese

1/4 cup diced red onion

3 tablespoons vegetable oil

6 tablespoons Cantaloupe Pesto

DIRECTIONS

1. In a large mixing bowl, gently toss together the orzo, chickpeas, cucumber, feta, and onion.

2. In a small mixing bowl, whisk together the vegetable oil and Cantaloupe Pesto. Drizzle this over the orzo mixture, and then gently toss to incorporate.

3. Serve cold.

Once Upon a Pesto

While *pilaf* is common in Armenia, its roots are tied to India and Iran. The earliest form of the word *pilaf* comes from a word that means 'a dish of rice and meat.'

Just Right

If you prefer to make this *pilaf* the traditional way, you can use cooked long-grain white rice, and then mix all of the ingredients, except for the cucumber, with the cooked rice. Then, when serving, top with 1/4 cup chopped cucumber.

CHAPTER 22: IRAN
Onion Pesto
INSPIRED BY IRAN

FOLK *or* FAIRY — SAVORY

MAKES 1 3/4 CUPS

TELLTALE *and* TIME — BEGINNER — 2 MINUTES

JESSICA PAHOLSKY

The oldest known cultivation of onions dates back to about 7,000 years ago. Some believe this bulb vegetable first grew in Iran. Thereafter, onion cultivation spread fast, in part because onions are easy to grow. They also adapt well to different soils and climates.

INGREDIENTS

1/4 cup shelled walnuts

2 cups quartered sweet onion

1/2 cup fresh mint

1/4 cup blue cheese

1/2 cup butter beans, rinsed and drained

2 tablespoons olive oil

DIRECTIONS

1. Combine all of the ingredients in a food processor. Blend until the desired consistency forms.

2. If using a mortar and pestle, crush the walnuts until a fine crumb forms. Add the onion and mint, and mash until smooth. Mix in the remaining ingredients. Mash until the desired consistency forms.

3. Store pesto in an airtight container or jar in the refrigerator for up to one week. Use throughout the week in the next two recipes. Pesto can last in an airtight container in the freezer for up to six months.

Once Upon a Pesto

Since onions naturally leave little to no trace for archaeologists to dig up, the precise origins of these vegetables are unknown.

ONCE UPON A PESTO

Roast Beef Pinwheels

MADE WITH ONION PESTO

MAKES 12 SERVINGS

TELLTALE *and* TIME

INTERMEDIATE, 40 MINUTES

Jessica Paholsky

As a whole, kebabs (or kabobs) encompass various meat dishes that originated in the Middle East. One type of kebab popular in Iran is *kebab koobideh*, or *kobida*. It's made with ground lamb or beef and mixed with chopped onions. Another kebab variation is *shish kebab*.

INGREDIENTS

4 8-inch whole-wheat tortillas

8 slices roast beef

1/4 cup Onion Pesto

24 toothpicks

DIRECTIONS

1. On 1 tortilla, spread 1 tablespoon of Onion Pesto into a thin, even layer using the back side of a spoon.
2. Lay 2 slices of roast beef in a single layer on the tortilla.
3. Roll tightly, and then wrap in cling wrap and transfer to a plate.
4. Repeat steps 1 through 3 three more times.
5. Refrigerate the pinwheels for at least 30 minutes.
6. Remove the pinwheels from the cling wrap and slice into 24 pieces (6 pieces per tortilla), each about 1 inch wide.
7. Insert a toothpick through each piece to keep them from unrolling, and then serve.

Once Upon a Pesto

Iran's national dish is the *chelo-kebab*. This type of kebab is made with broiled marinated lamb or chicken and served with rice.

Just Right

To make these pinwheels *chelo-kebab*-style, follow steps 1 through 6. Then, at step 7, instead of using toothpicks, thread onto 4 wooden skewers 6 pinwheel pieces each.

ONCE UPON A PESTO

Naan Bread

MADE WITH ONION PESTO

MAKES 8 SERVINGS

TELLTALE and TIME

INTERMEDIATE, 1 HOUR

JESSICA PAHOLSKY

Naan is the word for 'bread' in Iran. It also refers to a specific type of bread that Persians enjoy with cheese or butter. Traditionally, this flatbread is oven baked and stuffed with some type of meat.

INGREDIENTS

1 cup warm water

1 tablespoon sugar

2 teaspoons active dry yeast

1/2 cup Onion Pesto

3 cups all-purpose flour

1/2 cup dried cranberries

DIRECTIONS

1. In a large mixing bowl, combine the water, sugar, and yeast. Let sit for 5 minutes, or until foamy.
2. Mix in the Onion Pesto and flour.
3. Fold in the dried cranberries.
4. Knead the mixture for 2 minutes, or until fully incorporated.
5. Transfer the dough to a lightly greased bowl and cover with a damp towel. Let rise in a warm place for 30 minutes, or until doubled in size.
6. Transfer the dough to a floured surface and divide evenly into 8 dough balls.
7. Roll each dough ball into 1/8 inch thick flatbreads.
8. Cook each flatbread in a large non-stick skillet over medium heat for 1 to 2 minutes, or until lightly golden, on each side.
9. Once each flatbread is cooked, transfer it to a wire cooling rack.
10. Repeat steps 8 through 9 until all eight flatbreads are cooked and slightly cooled.
11. Serve warm with butter or cheese.

Once Upon a Pesto

Naan was probably first made when yeast arrived in India. The bread was mentioned early on by an Indian poet and musician.

Just Right

If your *naan* becomes leftovers, you can reheat each piece for about 2 minutes in a toaster, instead of reheating in a microwave or oven.

CHAPTER 23: INDIA
Carrot Pesto
INSPIRED BY INDIA

FOLK or FAIRY — NUT-FREE, SAVORY

MAKES 2 CUPS

TELLTALE and TIME — BEGINNER, 2 MINUTES

JESSICA PAHOLSKY

Carrot farming is an important part of the economy in India. Though most often orange in color, during the 10th century, carrots in India were actually purple. The root vegetable not only varies in color, but also in its use. Some Indian recipes use carrots with rice, others with salads or desserts.

INGREDIENTS

1/4 cup sesame seeds

2 cups carrots (cut to 1-inch pieces, boiled, drained, and completely cooled)

1 tablespoon fresh ginger, chopped

1/4 cup nonfat Greek yogurt

1 teaspoon curry powder

3 tablespoons vegetable oil

DIRECTIONS

1. Combine all of the ingredients in a food processor. Blend until the desired consistency forms.

2. If using a mortar and pestle, crush the sesame seeds until a fine crumb forms. Add the carrots and ginger, and mash until smooth. Mix in the remaining ingredients. Mash until the desired consistency forms.

3. Store pesto in an airtight container or jar in the refrigerator for up to one week. Use throughout the week in the next two recipes. Pesto can last in an airtight container in the freezer for up to six months.

Once Upon a Pesto

Orange carrots may have originated in Holland during the 16th century when various colors of carrots were hybridized to produce the most common modern orange version.

ONCE UPON A PESTO

Ramen Salad

MADE WITH CARROT PESTO

MAKES 2 SERVINGS

TELLTALE and TIME
INTERMEDIATE, 15 MINUTES

JESSICA PAHOLSKY

In India, a popular snack is Maggi instant noodles. Top Ramen is another brand of instant noodles in India. This is interesting given India's culinary tradition of making every meal from scratch. Upon introduction, instant food was a new concept in Indian culture.

INGREDIENTS

For the topping:
1 tablespoon olive oil
1/2 cup cooked lentils
1/2 raw instant ramen noodle square, crumbled
salt and pepper to taste

For the dressing:
1/4 cup Carrot Pesto
1 tablespoon nonfat Greek yogurt
2 tablespoons rice vinegar
2 teaspoons honey

2 cups chopped bok choy
2 cups shredded purple cabbage
3/4 cup chopped red bell pepper

DIRECTIONS

1. In a small saucepan over medium heat, combine the olive oil, lentils, instant ramen, salt, and pepper. Toast, stirring occasionally, until the ramen begins to turn golden brown on the outside, about 7 minutes. Set aside.

2. In a small mixing bowl, whisk together the Carrot Pesto, yogurt, vinegar, and honey. Set aside.

3. In a medium mixing bowl, toss together the bok choy, cabbage, and bell pepper. Divide the salad in half onto two serving plates.

4. Drizzle the dressing over each salad, and then top with ramen mix before serving.

Once Upon a Pesto

The popularity of ramen in India can be attributed to Japan's increasing investment in the country as well as a growing awareness of Japanese cuisine.

Just Right

Since you won't be using the included ramen spice packet in this recipe, you can save it for later use. Some ideas include seasoning plain rice or making broth in a way similar to using bouillon.

Once Upon A Pesto

Coconut Barfi

MADE WITH CARROT PESTO

MAKES 18 SERVINGS

TELLTALE *and* TIME

INTERMEDIATE, 1 HOUR AND 20 MINUTES

JESSICA PAHOLSKY

Barfi is a no-bake, milk-based confectionery in India. Its name comes from the Persian word *barf*, which means 'snow.' *Barfi* are made in many shapes and flavors, but the most classic of all is coconut.

INGREDIENTS

3 tablespoons butter

1 14 ounce can nonfat sweetened condensed milk

4 cups unsweetened coconut flakes

1/4 cup Carrot Pesto

1 teaspoon cinnamon

DIRECTIONS

1. In a large saucepan over medium heat, melt the butter.
2. Add the condensed milk and coconut flakes. Stir until even in consistency. Remove from the heat.
3. Divide the coconut mixture in half. To one half, add the Carrot Pesto and stir until incorporated. To the remaining half, add the cinnamon, and stir until incorporated.
4. Line a 9-by-5-inch baking pan with parchment paper.
5. Spread the Carrot Pesto coconut mixture in the pan, and work with a rubber spatula until it's packed and flattened.
6. Add the cinnamon coconut mixture next, and work until packed and flattened.
7. Chill the pan in the refrigerator for 1 hour, and then slice (see Just Right).
8. Transfer to a serving plate by placing the serving plate top-side-down over the pan. Flip the pan and plate upside down, leaving the cinnamon coconut layer directly on the plate and the Carrot Pesto coconut layer on top.
9. Remove the parchment paper from the dish and serve.
10. Cover with cling wrap or transfer to an airtight container, and store for up to two weeks.

Once Upon a Pesto

Barfi flavors are enhanced with fruits, nuts, and spices. The most common spice used is cardamom.

Just Right

Cut the *barfi* in any way you desire. The most common shapes in India are square, diamond, and round shapes.

CHAPTER 24: RUSSIA

Cherry Pesto

INSPIRED BY RUSSIA

FOLK *or* FAIRY — SWEET

MAKES 1 ½ CUPS

TELLTALE *and* TIME — BEGINNER — 2 MINUTES

JESSICA PAHOLSKY

During the 13th century, cherries arrived in Vladimir, a town just over 100 miles from Moscow, Russia. This stone fruit was crossbred with ground cherries, producing a sweet-sour variation that was then named Vladimir cherry. Vladimir cherries still grow in Russia today.

INGREDIENTS

1/4 cup shelled almonds

2 cups sweet cherries, halved and pitted

1/2 cup cubed Brie cheese

1/4 cup sweetened coconut flakes

DIRECTIONS

1. Combine all of the ingredients in a food processor. Blend until the desired consistency forms.

2. If using a mortar and pestle, crush the almonds until a fine crumb forms. Add the cherries and mash until smooth. Mix in the Brie cheese and coconut. Mash until the desired consistency forms.

3. Store pesto in an airtight container or jar in the refrigerator for up to one week. Use throughout the week in the next two recipes. Pesto can last in an airtight container in the freezer for up to six months.

Once Upon a Pesto

There were five original varieties of Vladimir cherries, and four of those are still cultivated today. Every year, Russians celebrate the Savior of the Cherry Feast Day with games involving everything cherry—cherry-eating contests, shooting with cherry stones, and more.

ONCE UPON A PESTO

Oatmeal Bars

MADE WITH CHERRY PESTO

MAKES 12 SERVINGS

TELLTALE *and* TIME

INTERMEDIATE, 50 MINUTES

JESSICA PAHOLSKY

From a very young age, Russians often eat different types of porridge for breakfast. They call it *kasha*. It's a hot cereal made with grains such as oatmeal, wheat, or millet and cooked with either water or milk. In addition to its place on the breakfast menu, *kasha* is also eaten with cabbage soup or some main dishes.

INGREDIENTS

2 cups old-fashioned oats

1 teaspoon baking powder

1 large ripe banana, mashed (3/4 cup)

1/2 cup Cherry Pesto

2 tablespoons fresh chopped sage

DIRECTIONS

1. Heat oven to 375° F.
2. Line an 8-by-8-inch pan with foil and grease lightly.
3. In a food processor, blend 1 cup rolled oats until a powder texture forms. Transfer to a medium-sized mixing bowl.
4. Add to the bowl the remaining rolled oats and baking powder. Mix together.
5. Add the mashed banana, Cherry Pesto, and sage. Stir until a dough forms, and let sit for 10 to 15 minutes to absorb the moisture.
6. Transfer the dough to the prepared pan, using a spatula to smooth it into an even layer.
7. Bake for 25 minutes, or until the edges begin to turn golden brown.
8. Let cool in the pan for 10 minutes.
9. Transfer the oatmeal bars to a wire cooling rack by placing the rack top-side-down on top of the pan and then flip it over. Let cool completely.
10. Cut the oatmeal bars into squares, and serve or store in an airtight container in the refrigerator for 1 to 2 weeks.

Once Upon a Pesto

Kasha is popular in Russia because not only is it easy to make, but also it's well-suited for preparing in large batches.

Just Right

If you prefer oatmeal bars to be thinner, use a 9-by-9-inch pan instead of an 8-by-8-inch pan.

Marshmallows

MADE WITH CHERRY PESTO

Once Upon a Pesto

The consistency of *zefir* is like that of marshmallows, but the shape is more similar to traditional meringue, a candy found in several European nations like Switzerland and France.

MAKES 15 TO 20 SERVINGS

TELLTALE and TIME

ADVANCED, 1 HOUR

JESSICA PAHOLSKY

Similar to marshmallows, a common confectionery made in Russia is called *zefir*. It got its name from the Greek god of the light west wind Zephyr. The light and airy consistency of this sweet is made by whipping fruit and berry purée with sugar, egg whites, and pectin or gelatine.

INGREDIENTS

2 envelopes Knox

1 cup cold water

1 3/4 cup sugar

1/4 cup Cherry Pesto

1/4 teaspoon salt

1/2 cup powdered sugar

1/3 cup semi-sweet chocolate chips

1 teaspoon coconut oil

DIRECTIONS

1. In a small mixing bowl, combine the Knox and 1/2 cup cold water. Set aside.
2. In a medium saucepan, combine the sugar, remaining water, and Cherry Pesto. Cook, stirring constantly, over medium-high heat until the sugar dissolves.
3. Add the Knox mixture to the pan. Bring to a boil, and then remove from the heat.
4. Stir in the salt.
5. Transfer the mixture to an electric mixing bowl. Mix on low for 3 to 4 minutes, or until the mixture is no longer steaming. Then, mix on high for 10 to 15 minutes, or until the mixture has doubled in size.
6. Sift a thin layer of powdered sugar into an 8-by-8-inch pan. Then, transfer the mixture from the electric mixing bowl to the pan in an even layer. Let cool completely.
7. Sift the remaining powdered sugar over the mixture in the pan.
8. Cut the marshmallows into the desired shape.
9. In a microwave-safe dish, combine the chocolate chips and coconut oil.
10. Microwave for 40 seconds, stirring halfway.
11. Transfer the chocolate mixture to a Ziploc bag, seal, and cut a 1/8-inch corner off one end.
12. Squeeze the chocolate mixture to the open corner of the Ziploc bag and drizzle the chocolate mixture over the cut marshmallows in a diagonal and then criss-cross pattern.
13. Serve. Cover any leftover marshmallows with cling wrap or transfer to an airtight container, and store in the refrigerator for 1 to 2 weeks.

Just Right

Be sure to whip the marshmallow batter for the full specified durations. Not whipping enough results in soggy, leaky, or dense marshmallows.

CHAPTER 25: CHINA
Spinach Pesto
INSPIRED BY CHINA

FOLK *or* FAIRY — NUT-FREE, SAVORY

MAKES 1 1/2 CUPS

TELLTALE *and* TIME — BEGINNER, 2 MINUTES

Jessica Paholsky

Spinach is not often linked with Chinese food in foreign cultures. Yet, ever since the 7th century when the King of Nepal sent it to China as a gift, the leafy green has been a staple in Chinese kitchens. Spinach is used in anything from broth bowls to stir-fry dishes. It also grows in many varieties in China. One variety is called *en choy*, which means 'Chinese spinach.'

INGREDIENTS

1/4 cup sunflower seeds

2 whole artichoke hearts

3 garlic cloves, peeled

1 8-ounce bag baby spinach

1/2 cup grated Asiago cheese

3 tablespoons olive oil

DIRECTIONS

1. Combine all of the ingredients in a food processor. Blend until the desired consistency forms.

2. If using a mortar and pestle, crush the sunflower seeds until a fine crumb forms. Add the artichoke, garlic, and spinach. Mash until fairly smooth. Mix in the remaining ingredients. Mash until the desired consistency forms.

3. Store pesto in an airtight container or jar in the refrigerator for up to one week. Use throughout the week in the next two recipes. Pesto can last in an airtight container in the freezer for up to six months.

Once Upon a Pesto

Spinach traces its roots to ancient Persia, which is present-day Iran. There, it was known as *aspanakh*.

ONCE UPON A PESTO

Stir-Fried Cauliflower Rice

MADE WITH SPINACH PESTO

MAKES 6 SERVINGS

TELLTALE and TIME

INTERMEDIATE, 30 MINUTES

JESSICA PAHOLSKY

Stir fry originated in China. During the Ming Dynasty, this technique for cooking meat and vegetables became widely popular among Chinese people. That's also when China's population doubled, and a growth in trade cultivated ties with the western world. As a result, stir fry spread to other areas of the world.

INGREDIENTS

3 tablespoons olive oil

2 eggs, beaten

1/2 cup chopped red bell pepper

1/2 cup chopped baby carrots

1/2 cup whole yellow corn kernels

1/2 cup frozen sweet peas

1/2 cup chopped red onion

2 tablespoons soy sauce

1 teaspoon rice vinegar

1 small head cauliflower

1/3 cup Spinach Pesto

1/2 cup chopped scallions

DIRECTIONS

1. Heat 1 tablespoon of olive oil in a small pan over medium heat. Add the eggs. Cook until the egg turns a light gold, about 5 minutes. Remove from the heat and chop the egg with a spatula into small pieces. Set aside.

2. In the same pan over medium-high heat, add 1 tablespoon of olive oil, the red bell pepper, carrots, corn, peas, and red onion. Cook for 5 minutes, stirring occasionally.

3. Add the soy sauce and rice vinegar. Cook for another 5 minutes. Remove from the heat and set aside.

4. Rinse the cauliflower with water to clean, remove the stems and leaves, and break the cauliflower into smaller pieces.

5. In a large food processor, pulse the cauliflower pieces for 10 seconds, until a rice-like texture forms.

6. In a large pan over medium-high heat, add the cauliflower rice, Spinach Pesto, and the remaining olive oil. Stir to incorporate. Cover and let cook for 7 minutes, stirring every 2 to 3 minutes.

7. Add the egg and the vegetable mixtures to the cauliflower mixture. Stir and cook for 2 minutes.

8. Serve with freshly chopped scallions on top.

Once Upon a Pesto

Stir frying originated in China, but it was not as important as boiling or steaming since the oil it required was considered expensive at that time. Stir frying became popular because it cooked food more quickly than other methods, which helped save fuel.

Just Right

The secret culinary tool for every Chinese stir-fry chef is a wok. The trick to using a wok for stir fry is to let it heat up for at least 2 minutes before adding any ingredients.

Chicken Dumplings
MADE WITH SPINACH PESTO

MAKES 8 SERVINGS

TELLTALE *and* TIME
ADVANCED, 40 MINUTES

Once Upon a Pesto
Though popular throughout South Asia, *momo*, or 'dumpling,' is believed to have originated in Tibet, where traveling merchants adapted the recipe ingredients, but kept its name.

JESSICA PAHOLSKY

Momo, or a type of steamed dumpling, is one of the most common foods in Nepal, the country that introduced China to spinach. In both Nepal and China, dumplings can be filled with meat or vegetables, steamed or fried, and served with different dipping sauces.

INGREDIENTS

For the dough:

2 cups flour, plus extra for dusting

1 cup water

For the filling:

1 pound ground chicken

1/3 cup chopped radicchio

1/4 cup chopped onion

1/3 cup Spinach Pesto

1 teaspoon ground fresh chili paste

Just Right

Traditional bamboo steamers don't get as hot as metal steamers, so dumplings are less likely to stick or get crispy from touching a bamboo steamer's insert. You can use either type of steamer when making these dumplings.

DIRECTIONS

1. In a medium-size mixing bowl, combine the flour and water until an elastic dough forms.
2. Round the dough into a ball. Cover it with plastic wrap. Set aside.
3. In another medium-size mixing bowl, combine the filling ingredients. Stir until incorporated.
4. Transfer the dough to a lightly floured surface. Using a rolling pin, roll the dough until it is 1/8 inch thick.
5. Cut the dough into circles using a cup or mug about 3 inches in diameter. Gather any excess dough and reshape into a ball.
6. Continue rolling the dough and cutting it into circles until as much of the dough is used as possible.
7. Fill the base of a steamer pot with 1 inch of water, leaving out the steamer insert. Bring the water to a boil over medium-high heat.
8. Meanwhile, transfer 1 tablespoon of the chicken mixture to the center of a dough circle.
9. Fold up the sides of the dough circle and pinch the dough in the center to close it into a dumpling shape.
10. Repeat steps 7 through 8 with all of the dough circles and chicken mixture.
11. Grease the top surface of the steamer insert (where the dumplings will rest) with oil and place it in the pot.
12. Add the dumplings to the pot with enough space so they do not touch each other.
13. Cover and steam for 10 minutes.
14. Transfer the cooked dumplings to a plate.
15. Repeat steps 12 through 14 until all of the dumplings have been cooked, adding oil to the base of the steamer insert if the dumplings begin to stick.
16. Let the cooked dumplings cool for at least 5 minutes before serving.

ONCE UPON A PESTO

CHAPTER 26: KOREA
Celery Pesto
INSPIRED BY KOREA

FOLK or FAIRY
DAIRY-FREE, SAVORY

MAKES 1 1/4 CUPS

TELLTALE and TIME
BEGINNER — 2 MINUTES

JESSICA PAHOLSKY

Celery has been cultivated since ancient times. The oldest cultivated form of celery is leaf celery, which traces its roots to East Asia. Common uses of celery in the East Asian peninsula of Korea include salads and *kimchi,* a popular fermented ethnic food.

INGREDIENTS

1/2 cup shelled peanuts

2 cups chopped celery (or 3 stalks)

1/4 cup chopped scallion (or 1 stalk)

2 garlic cloves, peeled

1 hard-boiled egg, peeled

1 tablespoon sesame oil

DIRECTIONS

1. Combine all of the ingredients in a food processor. Blend until the desired consistency forms.

2. If using a mortar and pestle, crush the peanuts until a fine crumb forms. Add the celery, scallion, and garlic, and mash until smooth. Mix in the remaining ingredients. Mash until the desired consistency forms.

3. Store pesto in an airtight container or jar in the refrigerator for up to one week. Use throughout the week in the next two recipes. Pesto can last in an airtight container in the freezer for up to six months.

Once Upon a Pesto

Celery gained popularity during the late 19th century when methods for growing the vegetable improved. At the same time, celery became available at moderate prices.

ONCE UPON A PESTO

171

Korean Egg Roll

MADE WITH CELERY PESTO

MAKES 2 SERVINGS

TELLTALE and TIME

INTERMEDIATE, 10 MINUTES

JESSICA PAHOLSKY

Egg rolls in Korean cuisine are much different from Chinese egg rolls. A Korean egg roll is literally egg cooked in a thin layer, like a *crêpe*, and then rolled. It's also similar to an omelet in that it's flavored with various mix-ins.

INGREDIENTS

3 eggs

1 tablespoon milk

3 tablespoons Celery Pesto

salt and pepper to taste

DIRECTIONS

1. In a medium-sized mixing bowl, whisk together all of the ingredients.
2. Lightly grease a frying pan and warm over medium heat. Once warm, pour half of the egg mixture into the pan. Swirl the pan to evenly distribute the egg into a thin layer. Cook until half done, about 1 minute.
3. Using a spatula, roll the egg tightly from right to left into a cylinder.
4. Pour half of the remaining egg mixture into the open part of the pan. Swirl to evenly distribute the egg on the right side of the rolled portion.
5. Cook for another 1 minute. Then using the spatula roll the rolled portion over the newly cooked egg from left to right.
6. Pour the rest of the egg mixture into the pan on the left side of the rolled portion. Swirl to distribute, then cook for 1 minute more.
7. Using the spatula, roll the rolled portion over the newly cooked egg from right to left.
8. Transfer the egg roll to a plate.
9. Let sit for 2 minutes before slicing into 1-inch-wide pieces, and serve at room temperature.

Once Upon a Pesto

Gyeran mari is the name for Korean egg roll. *Gyeran* means 'egg' and *mari* means 'rolled.' Korean egg roll is usually served as a side dish.

Just Right

Popular ways to eat Korean egg roll are in lunchboxes, as a snack, and during Korean happy hour.

ONCE UPON A PESTO

Millet Burgers

MADE WITH CELERY PESTO

MAKES 6 SERVINGS

TELLTALE and TIME

INTERMEDIATE, 1 HOUR

Jessica Paholsky

In Korea, millet has been an important ancient grain since about 3500 BC. While rice is Korea's most common grain, many Korean rice dishes mix in millet. Millet is also eaten for breakfast as a porridge.

INGREDIENTS

4 ounces button mushrooms, cooked in 2 tablespoons olive oil for 10 minutes

1 cup cooked millet

1/2 cup Celery Pesto

1 tablespoon ground flaxseed, mixed with 2 tablespoons water and let sit for 5 minutes

1/2 cup flour

DIRECTIONS

1. Heat oven to 350° F.
2. In a food processor, blend the mushrooms until meal-like, but not puréed.
3. In a large mixing bowl, combine the mushroom mixture with the remaining ingredients. Cover and let sit for 30 minutes.
4. Divide the mixture into six portions. Shape each portion into a patty about 1 inch thick. Transfer each millet patty to a greased cookie sheet.
5. Bake for 20 minutes, or until lightly browned on the outside.
6. Serve on a toasted multigrain roll.

Once Upon a Pesto

Developing countries in Asia and Africa account for the majority of the world's millet production. This crop thrives in hot and dry climates, and it's considered highly profitable.

Just Right

Millet, much like quinoa, is considered healthier than rice because it is richer in protein and fiber, making it a great vegan or vegetarian option.

CHAPTER 27: JAPAN
Daikon Pesto
INSPIRED BY JAPAN

FOLK *or* FAIRY
NUT-FREE, DAIRY-FREE, SAVORY

MAKES 1 1/2 CUPS

TELLTALE *and* TIME
BEGINNER — 2 MINUTES

JESSICA PAHOLSKY

Daikon is also known as Japanese radish or true daikon. It's a white radish, and its name literally means 'great root' in Japanese. People in Japan find many culinary uses for this root vegetable, from pickling, simmering, or drying daikon to grating it into a soy sauce.

INGREDIENTS

2 cups cubed daikon radish

2 scallions, chopped

1/4 cup chopped fresh dill

2 tablespoons fresh lemon juice

2 tablespoons honey

2 tablespoons soy sauce

DIRECTIONS

1. Combine all of the ingredients in a food processor. Blend until the desired consistency forms.

2. If using a mortar and pestle, mash the daikon, scallions, and dill until smooth. Mix in the remaining ingredients. Mash until the desired consistency forms.

3. Store pesto in an airtight container or jar in the refrigerator for up to one week. Use throughout the week in the next two recipes. Pesto can last in an airtight container in the freezer for up to six months.

Once Upon a Pesto

Grated daikon is another common way people in Japan eat this root vegetable. It usually accompanies fish dishes, and it's also used as a condiment to enhance the flavor of dishes like udon and soba noodles.

Sushi Stack

MADE WITH DAIKON PESTO

MAKES 8 SERVINGS

TELLTALE and TIME

INTERMEDIATE, 45 MINUTES

JESSICA PAHOLSKY

Alongside the cultivation of rice 2,000 years ago, the Japanese were crafting *sushi*. The first version developed as a means to preserve fish using fermented rice. Centuries later, people started to eat fish and rice together.

INGREDIENTS

1 cup jasmine rice

1/4 cup Daikon Pesto

2 ripe avocados, peeled and seeds removed

1 teaspoon wasabi powder

1 small cucumber, finely chopped

1 honeycrisp apple, cored and finely chopped

Toasted sesame seeds for garnish

DIRECTIONS

1. Cook the rice according to package directions.
2. Remove the cooked rice from the stove-top and immediately add the Daikon Pesto. Stir to incorporate. Set aside to cool.
3. Meanwhile, in a small bowl, mash together the avocados and wasabi powder. Set aside.
4. In another small bowl, toss together the cucumber and apple. Set aside.
5. Place a measuring cup or emptied soup can vertically onto a serving dish. Scoop 1/4 cup of the rice mixture into the bottom of the cup or can, and press it to form a flat top surface.
6. Next, transfer 1/8 of the avocado mixture into the cup or can on top of the rice, pressing to form a flat top surface.
7. Finally, scoop 1/8 of the apple mixture on top of the avocado and form it into a mound. Carefully remove the cup or can by lifting it straight up.
8. Sprinkle with sesame seeds.
9. Serve, or refrigerate for up to 2 days.

Once Upon a Pesto

Even though *sushi* is extremely popular in the history and present culture of Japan, the dish originated as a Chinese dish called *narezushi*. It was during the 8th century that *sushi* traveled from China to Japan.

Just Right

If your grocery store or local specialty food store carries it, an alternative to toasted sesame seeds as a garnish is *furikake*, a Japanese rice seasoning made of toasted sesame seeds, salt, and shredded toasted nori.

ONCE UPON A PESTO

Edamame

MADE WITH DAIKON PESTO

MAKES 8 SERVINGS

TELLTALE *and* TIME

INTERMEDIATE, 15 MINUTES

Jessica Paholsky

The first documented reference to *edamame* was made during the 13th century. It can be found in a Japanese monk's thank-you note written to his parishioner, who gave the monk a gift of these pod-enclosed soybeans. Today in Japan, *edamame* is a popular snack.

INGREDIENTS

1 16-ounce bag frozen edamame, thawed

2 tablespoons olive oil

1/3 cup Daikon Pesto

salt and pepper to taste

DIRECTIONS

1. Bring a medium pot of water to a boil over medium-high heat.
2. Cook the edamame in the boiling water for 5 minutes. Immediately drain and rinse under cold, running water. Pat dry.
3. Heat the olive oil in a large pan over medium heat.
4. Add the edamame and cook for 4 minutes, tossing occasionally
5. Add the Daikon Pesto, salt, and pepper. Toss to incorporate. Cook for another 3 minutes.
6. Serve hot.

Once Upon a Pesto

The Japanese word *edamame* means 'beans on a branch.'

Just Right

You can grow your own *edamame* in your summer garden. Like lima beans, *edamame* should not be eaten raw.

Once Upon A Pesto

CHAPTER 28: MALAYSIA

Lemongrass Pesto

INSPIRED BY MALAYSIA

FOLK *or* FAIRY — DAIRY-FREE, SAVORY

MAKES 1 1/4 CUPS

TELLTALE *and* TIME — BEGINNER, 2 MINUTES

JESSICA PAHOLSKY

Lemongrass is a common ingredient in Malaysia. As its name suggests, this grass-like herb has the flavor and aroma of lemon. The tender, white part closest to the stem is often thinly sliced and eaten raw with salads or cooked in simmered dishes. But, along with ginger, lemongrass has also been considered medicinal among some Asian cultures.

INGREDIENTS

- 1/4 cup shelled unsalted peanuts
- 2 small peaches, pitted and sliced
- 1 tablespoon chopped ginger
- 1 tablespoon chopped lemongrass
- 2 tablespoons olive oil

DIRECTIONS

1. Combine all of the ingredients in a food processor. Blend until the desired consistency forms.

2. If using a mortar and pestle, crush the peanuts until a fine crumb forms. Add the peaches and ginger, and mash until smooth. Mix in the lemongrass and olive oil. Mash until the desired consistency forms.

3. Store pesto in an airtight container or jar in the refrigerator for up to one week. Use throughout the week in the next two recipes. Pesto can last in an airtight container in the freezer for up to six months.

Once Upon a Pesto

In the world of medicine, lemongrass can be used to help digestive issues, high blood pressure, the common cold, aches, and exhaustion. Please consult your physician before using lemongrass in any of these ways.

Once Upon A Pesto

183

Kuih Puffs

MADE WITH LEMONGRASS PESTO

MAKES 8 SERVINGS

TELLTALE and TIME
ADVANCED, 1 HOUR

Jessica Paholsky

Kuih, or *kuih-muih* in plural, is bite-sized food in Malaysia. The word, which is pronounced kway, encompasses cakes, confections, and more. Most *kuih-muih* are sweet and eaten as dessert, but some are savory.

INGREDIENTS

1/2 cup butter

1/4 teaspoon salt

1 cup water

1 cup flour

4 eggs

1 egg yolk

2 cups heavy whipping cream

1/2 cup Lemongrass Pesto

Powdered sugar and cinnamon for garnish

DIRECTIONS

1. Heat oven to 400° F.
2. In a medium saucepan over medium heat, combine the butter, salt, and water. Cook, stirring constantly, until the butter has melted and begins to bubble.
3. Remove from the heat. Add the flour and stir. Let sit to cool for 5 minutes.
4. One at a time, add the eggs, and stir.
5. On a greased cookie sheet, drop 1/4-cup scoops of the batter with 3 inches of space between each.
6. Lightly brush the egg yolk on the top surfaces of each batter drop.
7. Bake for 30 minutes.
8. Cut each puff in half, hamburger-style, and let cool for at least 10 minutes.
9. Meanwhile, in a large mixing bowl, beat the heavy whipping cream until thickened, about 5 minutes.
10. Add the Lemongrass Pesto and continue beating for 1 minute more.
11. Immediately before serving, divide the whipped filling among the puffs, and sandwich each together.
12. Dust each puff with powdered sugar and cinnamon.

Once Upon a Pesto

Over the years, *kuih-muih* have been influenced by the migration of Chinese, Indian, and other cultures to Malaysia. This has led to different forms of *kuih-muih*.

Just Right

When beating the heavy whipping cream, it's important not to overbeat. Overbeating causes the whipped cream to become buttery.

ONCE UPON A PESTO

Shrimp Satay

MADE WITH LEMONGRASS PESTO

MAKES 3 TO 4 SERVINGS

TELLTALE *and* TIME

INTERMEDIATE, 40 MINUTES

JESSICA PAHOLSKY

Satay, or *sate* in Malay, is most akin to the kebab. It's made with meat threaded onto a wooden skewer that's then grilled over a fire and served with a peanut sauce in Southeast Asian countries like Malaysia. Both Malaysia and Thailand claim this dish as their own.

INGREDIENTS

1/4 cup Lemongrass Pesto

1 tablespoon peanut butter

1/2 teaspoon curry powder

1/8 teaspoon salt

1/2 pound shrimp, peeled and deveined

Jalapeños, parsley, red onion, and sesame seeds for garnish

DIRECTIONS

1. Heat oven to 475° F.
2. In a medium mixing bowl, combine the Lemongrass Pesto, peanut butter, curry powder, and salt. Stir until incorporated.
3. Gently toss the shrimp in the sauce until coated. Cover and let marinate for 10 to 15 minutes.
4. Meanwhile, soak 5 wooden skewers in water for 10 minutes.
5. Carefully thread 3 to 4 shrimp onto each skewer. Transfer the prepared skewers to a greased cookie sheet.
6. Bake for 6 to 8 minutes, or until lightly browned.
7. Garnish with jalapeños, parsley, red onion, and sesame seeds before serving.

Once Upon a Pesto

Many people around the world enjoy *satay* today. While it's considered a delicacy in Malaysia, Thailand, Singapore, and the Philippines, the dish is also popular in Thai and Malaysian restaurants in the United States.

Just Right

The most common version of *satay* is made with chicken. Use leftover cooked chicken breasts cut into 1-inch cubes instead of shrimp in this recipe, if you prefer.

CHAPTER 29: THAILAND
Mango Pesto
INSPIRED BY THAILAND

FOLK or FAIRY — SWEET

MAKES 1 1/2 CUPS

TELLTALE and TIME — BEGINNER — 2 MINUTES

JESSICA PAHOLSKY

Thailand's capital, Bangkok, is also known as the Big Mango. The nickname is fitting because mango is a native fruit of Thailand. The Asian nation is also the fourth-largest producer of mango in the world. Thai people enjoy it at every meal, from salads to a popular dessert called mango sticky rice.

INGREDIENTS

1/4 cup shelled almonds

1 mango, peeled and seed removed

1/4 cup chopped fresh ginger

1/2 cup fresh mint

1/4 cup mascarpone cheese

DIRECTIONS

1. Combine all of the ingredients in a food processor. Blend until the desired consistency forms.

2. If using a mortar and pestle, crush the almonds until a fine crumb forms. Add the mango and ginger, and mash until smooth. Mix in the mint and mascarpone cheese. Mash until the desired consistency forms.

3. Store pesto in an airtight container or jar in the refrigerator for up to one week. Use throughout the week in the next two recipes. Pesto can last in an airtight container in the freezer for up to six months.

Once Upon a Pesto

Mangoes come in a wide variety in Thailand. In the west, they are most often sweet and yellow, whereas other areas grow a more tart and green mango.

Once Upon A Pesto

Red Pepper Salad

MADE WITH MANGO PESTO

MAKES 8 TO 10 SERVINGS

TELLTALE *and* TIME

BEGINNER, 10 MINUTES

JESSICA PAHOLSKY

Salads in Thailand usually consist of a meat, seafood, or noodle base rather than greens or raw vegetables, as seen in other cultures of the world. Thai salads fall into one of four categories based on the way the ingredients are prepared: *yam, tam, larb,* and *phla.*

INGREDIENTS

For the salad:

2 red bell peppers, seeded and sliced

2 cups cut snow peas

2 cups chopped red cabbage

4 scallions, chopped

For the vinaigrette:

3 tablespoons sesame oil

1/4 cup Mango Pesto

1/2 teaspoon Sriracha

DIRECTIONS

1. In a large mixing bowl, combine the salad ingredients. Toss together.
2. In a small mixing bowl, combine the vinaigrette ingredients. Whisk together.
3. Drizzle the vinaigrette over the salad and toss to incorporate.
4. Divide the salad among serving plates.

Once Upon a Pesto

Yam means 'to mix,' so this salad is a mixture of various tasty ingredients. *Tam* means 'to pound,' and one example of this salad is a famous green papaya salad. *Larb* is known for its dressing and is best described as a meat salad. Finally, *phla* incorporates lemongrass, mint, and some form of meat.

Just Right

This salad can be served right away, or refrigerate it until you're ready to serve it. Overnight refrigeration allows all of the flavors to meld together even more.

Yellow Chicken Curry

MADE WITH MANGO PESTO

MAKES 4 SERVINGS

TELLTALE *and* TIME

INTERMEDIATE, 1 HOUR

JESSICA PAHOLSKY

Curry is crucial to Thai kitchens. However, curry's origins are Indian. Thailand adopted this dish, but incorporated its own local ingredients. One noticeable difference is Thai curry delivers a taste sweeter than Indian curry.

INGREDIENTS

4 boneless, skinless chicken thighs, cut into bite-sized pieces

1 tablespoon curry powder

2/3 cup Mango Pesto

1/2 onion, finely chopped

1 tablespoon olive oil

1 cup chicken broth

1 cup water

2 cups chopped carrot

2 cups chopped cauliflower

DIRECTIONS

1. In a medium mixing bowl, combine the chicken, curry powder, and Mango Pesto. Toss to coat and let marinate for 20 minutes.

2. In a large saucepan over medium heat, combine the chicken mixture, onion, and olive oil. Stirring occasionally, cook until the onions turn translucent and the meat is cooked through, about 15 minutes.

3. Add the broth and water to the saucepan, and bring to a boil.

4. Add the carrot and cauliflower. Cook until the vegetables become tender, about 20 minutes.

5. Divide among serving bowls.

Once Upon a Pesto

The word curry comes from the Indian Tamil word *kari*, which means 'a sauce or soup eaten with rice.' Curries can fit into one of two categories, wet curry and dry curry, depending on the amount of sauce used.

Just Right

Traditional curries don't skimp on seasonings and spices. Add more flavor to this dish by garnishing it with a simple topping such as toasted sesame seeds, shredded coconut, or some fresh pomegranate seeds.

CHAPTER 30: MYANMAR

Lemon Pesto

INSPIRED BY MYANMAR

FOLK *or* FAIRY — SWEET

MAKES 1 1/4 CUPS

TELLTALE *and* TIME — BEGINNER — 2 MINUTES

JESSICA PAHOLSKY

Lemons are thought to have originated in Burma, which is known today as Myanmar. This citrus fruit was found growing wild and appeared to be a cross between bitter orange and citron. During the 2nd century, lemons made their way to Europe, Africa, and other Asian nations.

INGREDIENTS

1/4 cup shelled pistachios

1 cup fresh blackberries

1/2 medium lemon, ends removed and cut in half

1/4 cup unsweetened coconut flakes

2 tablespoons ricotta cheese

2 tablespoons honey

DIRECTIONS

1. Combine all of the ingredients in a food processor. Blend until the desired consistency forms.

2. If using a mortar and pestle, crush the pistachios until a fine crumb forms. Add the blackberries, lemon, and coconut. Mash until fairly smooth. Mix in the remaining ingredients. Mash until the desired consistency forms.

3. Store pesto in an airtight container or jar in the refrigerator for up to one week. Use throughout the week in the next two recipes. Pesto can last in an airtight container in the freezer for up to six months.

Once Upon a Pesto

When lemons reached Rome, Italy, they were considered quite rare. The wealthy used them for decoration as well as medicine for curing ailments such as nausea and motion sickness.

ONCE UPON A PESTO

Bamboo Shoots Salad

MADE WITH LEMON PESTO

MAKES 2 TO 4 SERVINGS

TELLTALE and TIME

BEGINNER, 10 MINUTES

Jessica Paholsky

Shrimp and bamboo shoots are key products in Myanmar's economy and culture. Firstly, shrimp farming is an important industry as a result of the country's more than 1,800 miles of coastline. Additionally, bamboo shoots are popular among the country's markets.

INGREDIENTS

2 8-ounce cans bamboo shoots in water, drained and sliced lengthwise

4 tablespoons Lemon Pesto

1 cup 61-70 count shrimp, pre-cooked and tails removed

1/4 cup diagonally-sliced green onions

DIRECTIONS

1. In a medium bowl, gently toss together the bamboo shoots and Lemon Pesto until coated.

2. Stir in the shrimp and onion.

3. Serve at room temperature if desired, or refrigerate for an hour to let it chill.

Once Upon a Pesto

Bamboo shoots are not only popular to eat in Myanmar, but also they are widely harvested throughout the nation. Monsoon rains promote their growth from early June through late September.

Just Right

For most, bamboo shoots can be bought canned. But, fresh bamboo shoots are incomparable in taste for those who have access to them.

Once Upon A Pesto

Tapioca Pudding

MADE WITH LEMON PESTO

MAKES 4 SERVINGS

TELLTALE *and* TIME

BEGINNER, 10 MINUTES

JESSICA PAHOLSKY

In Myanmar, *moh let saung* is a dessert similar to tapioca pudding. It's made with coconut milk and sago. Sago is a starch that comes from palm trees. Sometimes, tapioca is used in sago's place. They are both starches made from cassava.

INGREDIENTS

1/3 cup large pearl tapioca

1 cup milk

1 13.5-ounce can coconut milk

pinch of salt

1/3 cup Lemon Pesto

DIRECTIONS

1. Combine the tapioca and milk in a medium saucepan. Soak for 30 minutes.
2. Add the coconut milk and salt. Bring to a boil over medium heat.
3. Reduce the heat and simmer for 20 minutes, stirring every 1 to 2 minutes.
4. Remove from the heat and stir in the Lemon Pesto until incorporated.
5. Transfer the pudding to a bowl or container to cool.
6. Chill overnight in the refrigerator before serving.

Once Upon a Pesto

Sago's history dates back prior to rice. Long before rice became widespread in Asia, sago was the go-to source of starch. Now, sago is used in various ways, from being whole in desserts to being processed into a dough for dumplings.

Just Right

Traditional Myanmar recipes use palm sugar. In this recipe, coconut and honey in the Lemon Pesto provide a similar sweetness. If you prefer a sweeter dessert, add a couple tablespoons of sugar during step 4.

PART 4: Africa and Islands

Many cultures around the world hunted and gathered for food. These traditions coincided with diets mainly of fruit with some meat and fish. Soon grains, nuts, and more processed foods like honey made their way into mealtime. Africa was no exception to these hunter-gatherer practices. In fact, some may confirm that the earliest history of man is based in Africa, where humans lived based on adaptations to their diet.

Sauce Similarity in Africa

In North Africa, **chermoula** is a fresh herb sauce that is used as a marinade or a relish. It often flavors fish or other seafood. But, it also pairs with meat and vegetables. Similar to pesto Genovese, its main ingredient is one or more herbs. However, instead of basil, *chermoula* uses parsley and cilantro. It's also made with citrus and spices like cumin.

Algeria, Libya, Morocco, and Tunisia all feature this sauce in their cooking, but Morocco claims to be its birthplace. The origin of the name *chermoula* comes from one of Morocco's two official languages, Arabic. In Arabic, the verb *chermel* means 'to rub' or 'to marinade something with a spice mix.'

31. MOROCCO
32. NIGERIA
33. EGYPT
34. ETHIOPIA
35. UGANDA
36. MOZAMBIQUE
37. SOUTH AFRICA
38. AUSTRALIA
39. NEW ZEALAND
40. FIJI

Just as the history of man stretches way back in time, so does food production. The location was Northern Africa. This area offered rich sources of fish, animals, and plants. In drier parts of Africa, nomad tribes relied on animal farming as well as cereals and tubers that could survive in extreme weather. Some of these early crops were wheat, barley, sorghum, and yams. Many of these remain staple foods throughout Africa today.

As human travel became more common, geographic differences correlated directly with diverse diets. The more people migrated and traded products, the more new foods and flavors arose among African cultures. On the other hand, there are some key culinary similarities throughout Africa. For one, meat is not eaten very often on this continent. Also, cooking usually takes place outside or in another building, not in the main living quarters.

Among North, West, East, and Southern Africa, certain differences are more notable today. In Southern Africa, there's more variety of fruits and vegetables, but corn maintains its central place in the traditional meal. With Arabic and South Asian influences, East Africa provides a realistic view of the impact of trade and migration. In West Africa, other starches like cassava and yam add a variety not seen in other parts of the continent. Finally, in North Africa—where it may have all started—Islamic traditions guide diets and many dishes reflect Mediterranean culture.

Across the ocean, the cuisines of Oceania include those of Australia, New Zealand, Fiji, and other islands. As in Africa, though these nations are separated by water, each culture continues to practice culinary traditions while adopting new ideas. Such practices are largely affected by the climate and resources available to each culture. With coastlines on all sides, these nations' diets are rich in seafood and often served with starches.

ONCE UPON A PESTO

201

CHAPTER 31: MOROCCO
Spices Pesto
INSPIRED BY MOROCCO

FOLK or FAIRY — DAIRY-FREE, SAVORY

MAKES 1 ½ CUPS

TELLTALE and TIME — BEGINNER, 2 MINUTES

202

JESSICA PAHOLSKY

Moroccan dishes feature flavors common among Mediterranean and Arabic cultures. Spices, in particular, take on a pretty serious role in this North Africa nation. They fill Moroccan markets, and combining spices into unique mixtures has no limit. One commonly used spice blend, called *ras el hanout*, consists of 27 different spices.

INGREDIENTS

1 tablespoon pine nuts

2 cups fresh parsley

2 garlic cloves, peeled

1 teaspoon peeled fresh ginger

2 teaspoons fresh lemon juice

4 tablespoons olive oil

1/2 teaspoon each: salt, cumin, cinnamon, turmeric

DIRECTIONS

1. Combine all of the ingredients in a food processor. Blend until the desired consistency forms.

2. If using a mortar and pestle, crush the pine nuts until a fine crumb forms. Add the parsley, garlic, and ginger, and mash until smooth. Mix in the remaining ingredients. Mash until the desired consistency forms.

3. Store pesto in an airtight container or jar in the refrigerator for up to one week. Use throughout the week in the next two recipes. Pesto can last in an airtight container in the freezer for up to six months.

Once Upon a Pesto

Some of the most commonly used spices in Morocco are cardamom, cumin, cloves, cinnamon, nutmeg, allspice, chili pepper, paprika, fenugreek, and turmeric.

Once Upon A Pesto

Couscous Salad

MADE WITH SPICES PESTO

MAKES 4 SERVINGS

TELLTALE and TIME

INTERMEDIATE, 10 MINUTES

JESSICA PAHOLSKY

Couscous is very popular in Morocco due to its simplicity and affordability. It's common for people to eat *couscous* on Fridays. This weekly tradition allows families to gather for a feast. And during these family feasts, *couscous* will be eaten with one's hand or with a spoon..

INGREDIENTS

1 cup cooked pearl couscous, cooked according to package directions

1/2 cup chopped granny smith apple

1/3 cup chopped and pitted kalamata olives

1/3 cup golden raisins

1 tablespoon Spices Pesto

1 tablespoon olive oil

DIRECTIONS

1. In a medium mixing bowl, combine the couscous, apple, olives, and raisins. Set aside.

2. In a small dish, whisk together the Spices Pesto and olive oil. Add this mixture to the couscous mixture. Gently toss until mixed throughout.

3. Serve, or store in an airtight container for up to 1 week.

Once Upon a Pesto

Couscous is the national dish of Morocco, Algeria, and Tunisia. From these North Africa countries, the dish then spread to other African nations and is now also popular in the Middle East.

Just Right

Couscous is cooked in a one-to-one liquid-to-*couscous* ratio. More often than not, this grain is more flavorful when cooked in broth, instead of water.

Lamb and Candied Fruit

MADE WITH SPICES PESTO

MAKES 4 SERVINGS

TELLTALE *and* TIME

INTERMEDIATE, 25 MINUTES

JESSICA PAHOLSKY

One of the most common meats in Morocco is lamb. Moroccan lamb has a different taste compared to Western lamb because of where sheep from various regions store their fat. The most common dish made with lamb in Morocco is called *tagine*. This dish is sweet, zesty, and usually made with fruit and nuts.

INGREDIENTS

1 pound butterflied leg of lamb

2 tablespoons butter

salt and pepper to taste

2 tablespoons Spices Pesto

2 tablespoons olive oil

1/3 cup chopped dried apricots

1/3 cup chopped and pitted dried dates

1 tablespoon sugar

DIRECTIONS

1. Cut the lamb into 1-inch cubes, and season with salt and pepper.
2. In a saucepan, melt 1 tablespoon of butter over medium heat.
3. Add the seasoned lamb cubes to the pan. Cook until browned on the outside and no longer pink in the middle, about 10 minutes.
4. Meanwhile in a small dish, combine the Spices Pesto and olive oil. Add this mixture to the lamb and toss to coat. Reduce the heat to a simmer, and cook for another 10 minutes.
5. In another pan over low heat, simmer the apricots, dates, sugar, and remaining 1 tablespoon of butter until soft and incorporated, about 2 minutes.
6. Remove both pans from the heat.
7. Transfer the lamb to serving plates and top with the candied fruit before serving.

Once Upon a Pesto

The word *tagine* is less about the stew and more about the pot that it's prepared in. An authentic clay *tagine* is a shallow glazed pot or bowl that holds all of the ingredients.

Just Right

Similar to beef, lamb can be prepared at more medium-rare temperatures. If you have a thermometer, that's 130° to 135° F. A well-done temperature is anywhere between 160° and 165° F.

CHAPTER 32: NIGERIA
Yam Pesto
INSPIRED BY NIGERIA

FOLK or FAIRY — SAVORY

MAKES 2 CUPS

TELLTALE and TIME — INTERMEDIATE, 30 MINUTES

JESSICA PAHOLSKY

Yam is sometimes called the king of crops in Nigeria. This African country is the world's largest producer of yams. Not only do Nigerians value the versatility of yams, but they also hold an annual celebration at the end of the farming season that honors this tuber. There are dances, parades, costumes, and many yam dishes to eat.

INGREDIENTS

1 small yam, peeled and cubed

2 cups chopped leek

1/2 orange, juiced

1 tablespoon butter

1/3 cup pecans

1/4 cup fresh thyme

1/4 cup olive oil

DIRECTIONS

1. In a large pan over medium heat, combine yam, leek, orange juice, and butter. Cover and let cook for 15 minutes, stirring occasionally to prevent browning.

2. Let cool for 5 to 10 minutes. Combine yam mixture with the remaining ingredients in a food processor. Blend until a smooth paste forms.

3. If using a mortar and pestle, crush the pecans until a fine crumb forms. Add the cooked yam mixture, and mash until smooth. Mix in the thyme and olive oil. Mash until the desired consistency forms.

4. Store pesto in an airtight container or jar in the refrigerator for up to one week. Use throughout the week in the next two recipes. Pesto can last in an airtight container in the freezer for up to six months.

Once Upon a Pesto

The origin of yams reflects religious beliefs shared among many. One common story is that yams were given to this world by a supreme being or god of various Nigerian subcultures.

Once Upon A Pesto

Plantain Bread

MADE WITH YAM PESTO

MAKES 16 SERVINGS

TELLTALE and TIME
INTERMEDIATE, 1 HOUR AND 30 MINUTES

JESSICA PAHOLSKY

Plantain, or banana's starchier sister, is a common ingredient in Nigerian cuisine. It is prepared as chips, blended into pudding, fried, and mashed. These various cooking methods developed and have been refined since plantains were first grown in eastern Africa as early as 3000 BC.

INGREDIENTS

1/2 cup butter

1 cup brown sugar

2 eggs

2 ripe plantains, peeled and mashed

1/2 cup Yam Pesto

2 cups flour

1/2 teaspoon baking powder

1/2 teaspoon baking soda

1/2 teaspoon salt

1/2 cup shelled chopped pecans

DIRECTIONS

1. Heat oven to 350° F.
2. In a large mixing bowl, cream together the butter and brown sugar.
3. One at a time, add the eggs and beat into the butter mixture.
4. Add the plantains and Yam Pesto to the butter mixture, and stir until incorporated.
5. In a separate bowl, mix together the flour, baking powder, baking soda, and salt. Then add it to the plantain mixture.
6. Stir until completely incorporated and a smooth, runny batter forms.
7. Fold in the pecans.
8. Transfer the batter into a greased bread loaf pan.
9. Bake for 50 to 60 minutes.
10. Remove the bread from the pan by inverting it onto a wire cooling rack. Let cool for at least 10 minutes before slicing.
11. Serve fresh, or refrigerate for up to 5 days in a Ziploc bag or airtight container.

Once Upon a Pesto

Dodo is a dish of fried sweet plantains popular not only in Nigeria, but also throughout Yoruba, a western African ethnic group among Nigeria, Benin, and Togo.

Just Right

The easiest way to peel a plantain is to cut off the ends with a paring knife. Then, score the skin so as to not cut into the flesh too far, and pry the skin off around the plantain.

Peanut Stew

MADE WITH YAM PESTO

MAKES 12 SERVINGS

TELLTALE and TIME

INTERMEDIATE, 1 HOUR

Jessica Paholsky

Peanut stew, which is also called groundnut soup or *maafe,* is a soup native to Nigeria and popular throughout West Africa. Peanuts reached Africa during the 16th century, and the people of Nigeria quickly adopted the new food into their culinary traditions.

INGREDIENTS

1 onion, peeled and chopped

1 tablespoon olive oil

2 tablespoons chopped fresh ginger

1 6-ounce can tomato paste

1/2 cup Yam Pesto

2 teaspoons ground coriander

1 teaspoon paprika

1 teaspoon salt

4 cups vegetable stock

20 okra pods, cut into 1/2-inch-thick pieces

1 small eggplant, cubed

1/2 cup shelled peanuts

DIRECTIONS

1. In a large pot over medium heat, combine the onion and olive oil. Stirring constantly, cook until the onion becomes translucent, about 10 minutes.

2. Add the ginger, tomato paste, Yam Pesto, coriander, paprika, and salt. Stir until incorporated.

3. Add the vegetable stock, and mix until a smooth broth forms, about 1 minute.

4. Add the okra, eggplant, and peanuts. Bring to a boil, and then reduce the heat to low and let simmer for 30 minutes, stirring occasionally.

5. Divide among serving bowls, and serve immediately.

Once Upon a Pesto

In many areas of Africa, peanuts are called groundnuts because the nut pods grow underground. With healthy fats and some protein, they play an important role in African diets.

Just Right

In Africa, peanut stew is prepared with meat like chicken, beef, or lamb. It's also often eaten with mashed yams or sweet potatoes. Add to and accompany this recipe as you prefer.

ONCE UPON A PESTO

CHAPTER 33: EGYPT
Olive Pesto
INSPIRED BY EGYPT

FOLK or FAIRY — NUT-FREE, SAVORY

MAKES 1 CUP

TELLTALE and TIME — BEGINNER, 2 MINUTES

JESSICA PAHOLSKY

Since 2500 BC, olives have been cultivated in the Mediterranean. Their early history occurs in Egypt and then travels north across the Mediterranean Sea to Italy. Centuries later, olives reached the New World and now are grown as far away from their origins as Asia and Australia.

INGREDIENTS

1 1/2 cups pitted olives

2 tablespoons chopped shallot

3 ounces feta cheese

2 tablespoons fresh lemon juice

1 tablespoon olive oil

DIRECTIONS

1. Combine all of the ingredients in a food processor. Blend until the desired consistency forms.

2. If using a mortar and pestle, mash the olives and shallot until smooth. Mix in the remaining ingredients. Mash until the desired consistency forms.

3. Store pesto in an airtight container or jar in the refrigerator for up to one week. Use throughout the week in the next two recipes. Pesto can last in an airtight container in the freezer for up to six months.

Once Upon a Pesto

Olives in ancient Egypt extended beyond food. For example, olive branches made into ornaments and crowns have been found in the tomb of King Tut, a famous ancient Egyptian pharaoh.

Once Upon A Pesto

Mediterranean Salad

MADE WITH OLIVE PESTO

MAKES 6 TO 8 SERVINGS

TELLTALE and TIME

INTERMEDIATE, 50 MINUTES

Jessica Paholsky

In Egypt, *meze* is the term that encompasses starters and salads served with bread prior to the main meal. One such salad is called *salata baladi*. It's made with tomatoes, cucumbers, onions, and other fresh flavorings.

INGREDIENTS

1 1/2 cups cut asparagus
2 teaspoons olive oil
3 cups chopped cucumber
2 cups chopped bell pepper (seeds removed)
2 cups chopped tomato
1 cup chopped onion
Feta cheese for garnish

For the vinaigrette:
2 tablespoon Olive Pesto
4 tablespoons olive oil
4 tablespoons red wine vinegar
1/2 teaspoon dried oregano
1/4 teaspoon dried dill
pinch of black pepper

DIRECTIONS

1. In a medium pan over medium-high heat, toss together the asparagus and olive oil. Cover and cook for 5 minutes.

2. Stir, cover, and cook for another 5 minutes, or until the asparagus is tender.

3. Transfer the cooked asparagus to a bowl, and chill for at least 30 minutes.

4. Meanwhile, combine the cucumber, bell pepper, tomato, and onion in a large bowl. Set aside.

5. Once the asparagus is chilled, toss with the cucumber mixture.

6. In a small bowl, combine the vinaigrette ingredients. Whisk together with a fork.

7. Drizzle the vinaigrette over the salad. Gently toss to incorporate.

8. Serve the salad topped with crumbled feta cheese as desired.

Once Upon a Pesto

Another use for olives in Egypt is olive oil. Egyptians used olive oil not only in their food, but also for lighting, medicine, and rituals.

Just Right

To make this salad into a meal, add in beans, legumes, grains, or meat.

ONCE UPON A PESTO

Mac 'N Cheese

MADE WITH OLIVE PESTO

MAKES 6 TO 8 SERVINGS

TELLTALE and TIME
INTERMEDIATE, 30 MINUTES

JESSICA PAHOLSKY

Some believe that cheese originated in the Middle East since jars dating to the First Dynasty of Egypt were found containing traces of it. While macaroni and cheese is likely from Europe, pasta, often in the form of elbow noodles, is a main ingredient in what some consider Egypt's national dish, *kushari*.

INGREDIENTS

1 16-ounce box cavatappi pasta

1 tablespoon olive oil

6 garlic cloves, peeled

3 cups baby spinach

3/4 cup plain Greek yogurt

8 ounces sharp white cheddar cheese

1/3 cup Olive Pesto

DIRECTIONS

1. Cook the cavatappi pasta following the package directions, drain, and set aside.
2. Meanwhile, in a large pan over medium-high heat, combine the olive oil and garlic.
3. Cook for 2 minutes. Toss and cook for 1 minute more.
4. Add the spinach to the garlic, and stir to combine.
5. Cook for 1 1/2 minutes, or until the spinach begins to wilt.
6. Remove the spinach from the heat and transfer to a bowl. Set aside.
7. In the large pan over low heat, combine the cooked pasta, Greek yogurt, cheddar cheese, and Olive Pesto. Stir to incorporate.
8. Continue stirring until the cheese fully melts, about 6 minutes.
9. Add the garlic and spinach mixture to the pan, and stir.
10. Cook for another 4 minutes.
11. Remove the pan from the heat and divide among serving bowls or plates.

Once Upon a Pesto

Kushari is prepared in nearly every restaurant and home in Egypt. Street vendors who sell this dish from their carts are fondly known as *kushari* men.

Just Right

This comfort food recipe is a great way to use pantry staples. *Kushari* is often served with tomato sauce, so pair this Mac 'N Cheese with stewed tomatoes on the side for a traditional Egyptian touch.

CHAPTER 34: ETHIOPIA
Okra Pesto
INSPIRED BY ETHIOPIA

FOLK or FAIRY
NUT-FREE, DAIRY-FREE, SAVORY

MAKES 1 ½ CUPS

TELLTALE and TIME
BEGINNER — 2 MINUTES

220

JESSICA PAHOLSKY

Okra, also known as lady fingers, is a pod-producing plant that originated in what is today Ethiopia. While it's categorized as a vegetable, its seeds are often toasted, ground, and then used as a coffee substitute. Another use for okra stems from its sticky juice, which can help thicken stews.

INGREDIENTS

2 cups chopped frozen okra, thawed and pat dry

2 garlic cloves, peeled

1/2 tablespoon chopped fresh ginger

1 Roma tomato, stem removed

2 tablespoons cornmeal

1/2 teaspoon ground cumin

1/2 teaspoon ground turmeric

1/4 teaspoon chopped dried chili pepper, or crushed red pepper flakes

DIRECTIONS

1. Combine all of the ingredients in a food processor. Blend until the desired consistency forms.

2. If using a mortar and pestle, mash the okra, garlic, ginger, and tomato until fairly smooth. Mix in the remaining ingredients. Mash until the desired consistency forms.

3. Store pesto in an airtight container or jar in the refrigerator for up to one week. Use throughout the week in the next two recipes. Pesto can last in an airtight container in the freezer for up to six months.

Once Upon a Pesto

As a member of the mallow family, which also includes cotton and hollyhock plants, okra provides another practical use. Old okra can be processed to make paper.

Stovetop Popcorn

MADE WITH OKRA PESTO

MAKES 4 SERVINGS

TELLTALE *and* TIME

BEGINNER, 15 MINUTES

JESSICA PAHOLSKY

One of the most recognizable parts of Ethiopian culture is a coffee ceremony called *buna tetu*. This tradition is important because receiving an invitation to a coffee ceremony is considered a sign of friendship and respect. Once the coffee has been made, the ceremony involves a snack such as popcorn.

INGREDIENTS

3 tablespoons olive oil

1/2 cup white popcorn kernels

1/4 cup Okra Pesto

DIRECTIONS

1. In a four-quart saucepan over medium heat, combine the olive oil and 3 popcorn kernels. Cover and cook until the 3 kernels pop.
2. Add the remaining popcorn kernels and cover.
3. As the kernels pop, move the saucepan back and forth.
4. Once the popping begins to slow, remove the saucepan from the heat and transfer the popcorn to a rimmed baking sheet.
5. Toss the cooked popcorn in the Okra Pesto until incorporated, and serve immediately.

Once Upon a Pesto

Sometimes, like the coffee that's served, the popcorn is sweetened with sugar. In addition to popcorn, coffee ceremonies can feature peanuts or traditional bread as the snack.

Just Right

If you plan to serve or eat this popcorn later, complete steps 1 through 4. Then, a few minutes before serving or eating, complete step 5. This prevents the popcorn from becoming soggy.

ONCE UPON A PESTO

Spiced Lentils

MADE WITH OKRA PESTO

MAKES 4 SERVINGS

TELLTALE and TIME

INTERMEDIATE, 45 MINUTES

JESSICA PAHOLSKY

In Ethiopia, *wat* is a spiced dish similar to a stew or curry. It can be made with legumes, such as lentils, or with meat, fish, or vegetables. The recipes for *wat* vary far and wide, from village to village and home to home.

INGREDIENTS

1 cup dried lentils

1 tablespoon olive oil

2 cups vegetable broth

1/2 cup Okra Pesto

Sour cream for garnish

DIRECTIONS

1. In a medium saucepan over medium heat, combine the lentils and olive oil. Cook for 2 minutes.

2. Add the vegetable broth and Okra Pesto, and bring to a boil.

3. Reduce the heat to low. Simmer, covered, for 25 minutes, stirring every 3 to 5 minutes.

4. Divide among serving dishes, and top with a dollop of sour cream.

Once Upon a Pesto

Misir wat is a version of *wat* made with red lentils, ground spices, common vegetables, and herbs.

Just Right

A traditional dish of lentil wat is served with a dollop of a*yib*, a fresh Ethiopian cheese. If you have access to this cheese, you can use it instead of a dollop of sour cream.

ONCE UPON A PESTO

CHAPTER 35: UGANDA

Banana Pesto

INSPIRED BY UGANDA

FOLK or FAIRY — NUT-FREE, DAIRY-FREE, SWEET

MAKES 1 3/4 CUPS

TELLTALE and TIME — BEGINNER, 2 MINUTES

JESSICA PAHOLSKY

Bananas are a staple in Uganda. From green bananas called *matooke* to fermented banana wine, Ugandans not only consume the most bananas per person—500 pounds per person per year—but this African country is also the world's largest banana producer.

INGREDIENTS

1 tablespoon sesame seeds

1 1/2 cups peeled ripe banana (or 2 small bananas)

1 1/2 cups quartered strawberries

1/2 cup orange slices

1/2 teaspoon ground cardamom

1/2 tablespoon honey

DIRECTIONS

1. Combine all of the ingredients in a food processor. Blend until the desired consistency forms.

2. If using a mortar and pestle, crush the sesame seeds until a fine crumb forms. Add the banana, strawberries, and orange, and mash until fairly smooth. Mix in the remaining ingredients. Mash until the desired consistency forms.

3. Store pesto in an airtight container or jar in the refrigerator for up to one week. Use throughout the week in the next two recipes. Pesto can last in an airtight container in the freezer for up to six months.

Once Upon a Pesto

Ugandan people do their best not to waste any part of the banana plant. They use banana leaves to make roofs and banana fibers to make clothing and handicrafts.

ONCE UPON A PESTO

Spiced Chicken

MADE WITH BANANA PESTO

MAKES 2 TO 4 SERVINGS

TELLTALE *and* TIME

INTERMEDIATE, 1 HOUR AND 20 MINUTES

Jessica Paholsky

Among some Ugandan people, meat is reserved for special celebrations. It may be chicken or beef and either roasted or grilled. Chicken in Uganda is often flavored with some salt and then some pineapple or lemon juice to accelerate the cooking time.

INGREDIENTS

4 chicken thighs, skin removed

1/2 tablespoon olive oil

1/4 cup chopped onion

1/4 cup chicken broth

1/4 cup Banana Pesto

1/2 teaspoon salt

1/4 cup golden raisins

DIRECTIONS

1. Heat oven to 350° F.
2. In a large pan over medium-high heat, combine the chicken thighs, bone-side up, and olive oil. Cook for 15 minutes, until golden brown on the non-bone side.
3. Remove the chicken thighs from the pan, and set aside.
4. In the same pan, over medium-low heat, cook the onion for 10 minutes, stirring occasionally to prevent browning.
5. Add the chicken broth, Banana Pesto, and salt. Cook for 2 minutes, stirring constantly, until slightly thickened.
6. Add the chicken thighs back to the pan.
7. Add the golden raisins, and cook for 1 minute more.
8. Transfer the chicken mixture to an 8-by-8-inch baking dish.
9. Bake for 40 minutes.
10. Let cool for 5 to 10 minutes before serving.

Once Upon a Pesto

In 2018 in Uganda, poultry consumption per capita was about one and a half kilograms. That same year, the country's banana consumption per capita was nearly 12 kilograms.

Just Right

To make a no-fuss quick dinner, you can skip browning the chicken. Go straight from step 1 to step 4.

Once Upon A Pesto

Cassava Muffins

MADE WITH BANANA PESTO

MAKES 8 SERVINGS

TELLTALE *and* TIME

INTERMEDIATE, 45 MINUTES

JESSICA PAHOLSKY

In addition to banana, other Ugandan staples include cassava, maize, and yam. Viewed as a reliable and affordable source of carbs, cassava didn't arrive in Uganda until the 19th century. Now, the starchy root appears worldwide in several consumable forms, including cassava flour.

INGREDIENTS

1 1/2 cups cassava flour (also known as tapioca flour)

2 tablespoons sugar

3/4 teaspoon baking powder

1/2 teaspoon baking soda

1/2 teaspoon salt

3/4 cup chocolate chips

1 cup Banana Pesto

1/2 cup vegetable oil

1 egg

DIRECTIONS

1. Heat oven to 350° F.
2. In a large mixing bowl, combine the flour, sugar, baking powder, baking soda, salt, and chocolate chips. Set aside.
3. In a small mixing bowl, whisk together the Banana Pesto, vegetable oil, and egg.
4. Add the Banana Pesto mixture to the dry ingredients.
5. Mix until combined. Let sit for 5 minutes.
6. Lightly grease or line with cupcake paper a muffin tin pan.
7. Divide the batter evenly among 8 muffin tins.
8. Bake for 20 to 25 minutes, or until the edges start to turn golden brown.
9. Transfer the cooked muffins to a wire cooling rack.
10. Let cool for at least 5 minutes before serving.

Once Upon a Pesto

Cassava has many other names around the globe. It's also called manioc, balinghoy, mogo, mandioca, tapioca root, and yuca. However, yucca—spelled with double "c"—is completely different from yuca and cassava.

Just Right

When filling muffin cups, it's best to aim for three-quarters full. This allows room for the muffins to rise without overflowing and making a mess while baking.

ONCE UPON A PESTO

CHAPTER 36: MOZAMBIQUE
Cassava Pesto
INSPIRED BY MOZAMBIQUE

FOLK or FAIRY — DAIRY-FREE, SAVORY

MAKES 1 1/2 CUPS

TELLTALE and TIME — BEGINNER, 2 MINUTES

Jessica Paholsky

Cassava, or sometimes known as yuca, is a starchy root used to make common food items like flour and tapioca. It was introduced to Africa by Portuguese traders from Brazil during the 16th century. In Mozambique, cassava is one of the most important starches.

INGREDIENTS

1/3 cup shelled cashews

1/2 cup peeled and cubed yuca root

2 yellow bell peppers, seeded and chopped

1 1/2 teaspoons cumin seeds (or 1 teaspoon cumin powder)

2 tablespoons fresh oregano

3 tablespoons lemon juice

DIRECTIONS

1. Combine all of the ingredients in a food processor. Blend until the desired consistency forms.

2. If using a mortar and pestle, crush the cashews until a fine crumb forms. Add the yuca, bell peppers, and cumin, and mash until smooth. Mix in the remaining ingredients. Mash until the desired consistency forms.

3. Store pesto in an airtight container or jar in the refrigerator for up to one week. Use throughout the week in the next two recipes. Pesto can last in an airtight container in the freezer for up to six months.

Once Upon a Pesto

Cassava is an important source of energy in Mozambique. Additionally, hundreds of millions of people rely on cassava as their primary food staple worldwide.

ONCE UPON A PESTO

233

Tomato Cobbler

MADE WITH CASSAVA PESTO

MAKES 8 TO 10 SERVINGS

TELLTALE and TIME

INTERMEDIATE, 1 HOUR AND 20 MINUTES

JESSICA PAHOLSKY

Cassava is used to make tapioca, which is processed into many forms, including flakes and pearls. Tapioca pearls are often used to help bind the filling in pies and cobblers. In addition to cassava's important role in Mozambique, cornmeal is another starch popular in Mozambican cooking.

INGREDIENTS

1 heirloom tomato, cored and chopped

1 pint cherry or grape tomatoes, halved

2 tablespoons tapioca

1 tablespoon olive oil

1 1/2 teaspoons salt

4 oz crumbled goat cheese

1/2 cup Cassava Pesto

1/3 cup flour

1/3 cup cornmeal

1 tablespoon brown sugar

5 tablespoons unsalted butter

DIRECTIONS

1. Heat oven to 375° F.
2. In a large mixing bowl, toss together the tomatoes, tapioca, olive oil, 1 teaspoon salt, goat cheese, and Cassava Pesto.
3. Transfer the tomato mixture to a greased 9-inch pie dish. Spread to form a flat layer.
4. In a food processor, combine the flour, corn meal, brown sugar, remaining salt, and butter. Pulse for 8 to 10 seconds. Spread evenly over the tomato mixture.
5. Bake for 55 to 60 minutes, or until the crust turns golden brown.
6. Transfer the pie dish to a wire cooling rack and let cool for 10 minutes before serving.

Once Upon a Pesto

One traditional dish in Mozambique also popular throughout Africa is *xima*. It's a type of porridge made with cornmeal and mild flavors.

Just Right

Depending on what produce is in season and what you may grow yourself, you can use any combination of fresh tomato varieties, so long as you maintain the same volume of tomatoes in this recipe.

ONCE UPON A PESTO

Watermelon Ceviche

MADE WITH CASSAVA PESTO

MAKES 8 SERVINGS

TELLTALE *and* TIME

BEGINNER, 2 HOURS AND 10 MINUTES

JESSICA PAHOLSKY

Claiming over 1,500 miles of the African coastline, Mozambique's cuisine offers plenty of seafood. One common recipe is a seafood stew made with clams in a peanut sauce. Another popular dish is shrimp prepared in the style of *peri-peri,* a word from Portuguese, which highlights Portugal's influence in Africa.

INGREDIENTS

1 4-ounce can jumbo squid pieces, drained and rinsed

2/3 cup lemon juice

1 teaspoon lemon zest

1/4 cup Cassava Pesto

2 cups cubed watermelon

1 cup baby spinach

DIRECTIONS

1. In a small mixing bowl, combine the squid, lemon juice, and lemon zest. Let marinate in the refrigerator for 2 hours.

2. After marinating, drain the excess lemon juice from the squid mixture.

3. Add the remaining ingredients to the squid mixture, and toss.

4. Serve cold.

Once Upon a Pesto

In addition to seafood being a popular food throughout Mozambique, it's also exported in great quantities. In 2020, for example, Mozambique shipped nearly 90,000 kilograms of squid and cuttlefish.

Just Right

Ceviche goes well with tortilla chips or crackers, eaten similar to a salsa. It can also be served like bruschetta, served atop toasted slices of baguette.

CHAPTER 37: SOUTH AFRICA
Corn Pesto
INSPIRED BY SOUTH AFRICA

FOLK *or* FAIRY
NUT-FREE, SAVORY

MAKES 1 ¼ CUPS

TELLTALE *and* TIME
BEGINNER — 2 MINUTES

JESSICA PAHOLSKY

Corn dominates South African cuisine. It's seen everywhere from a porridge called *mealie pap* to a salad made of maize meal. South Africans even have their own name for corn, *mealies*, and it's the most important grain crop in the country's economy.

INGREDIENTS

2 ears of raw corn, kernels removed (or 2 cups canned corn)

1 cup loosely packed fresh chervil (or curly parsley)

2 garlic cloves

2 tablespoons butter, melted

1/4 teaspoon salt

DIRECTIONS

1. Combine all of the ingredients in a food processor. Blend until the desired consistency forms.

2. If using a mortar and pestle, mash the corn, chervil, and garlic until smooth. Mix in the butter and salt. Mash until the desired consistency forms.

3. Store pesto in an airtight container or jar in the refrigerator for up to one week. Use throughout the week in the next two recipes. Pesto can last in an airtight container in the freezer for up to six months.

Once Upon a Pesto

Maize was brought to the African continent at the start of the 16th century. But, it wasn't until 1655 that the crop reached South Africa. Not long after that, corn took on its important role throughout the nation.

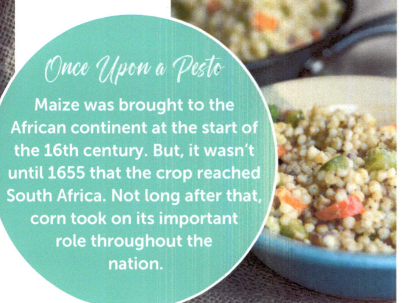

ONCE UPON A PESTO

Sorghum Pilaf

MADE WITH CORN PESTO

MAKES 4 SERVINGS

TELLTALE and TIME

INTERMEDIATE, 20 MINUTES

JESSICA PAHOLSKY

Both corn and sorghum are among South Africa's top five grain crops. Sorghum, a grain indigenous to Africa, is used in porridge, bread, beer, and livestock feed. The cereal can thrive on marginal land and in drier conditions, making it a reliable crop in many areas throughout Africa.

INGREDIENTS

4 chicken thighs, skin removed

1/2 tablespoon olive oil

1/4 cup chopped onion

1/4 cup chicken broth

1/4 cup Banana Pesto

1/2 teaspoon salt

1/4 cup golden raisins

DIRECTIONS

1. In a large skillet over medium-low heat, combine the bell peppers, onion, and olive oil. Cook for 10 minutes, stirring every couple of minutes to prevent browning.

2. Add the sorghum and Corn Pesto. Cook for 5 minutes, stirring to incorporate.

3. Remove the skillet from the heat, and stir in the lemon juice until incorporated.

4. Serve warm.

Once Upon a Pesto

Although sorghum has become less popular compared to other grains, South African human consumption of sorghum as food and beverage accounts for nearly 90 percent of the use of this grain.

Just Right

Cooking sorghum is much like cooking rice. However, the grain-to-water ratio for sorghum is one-to-three. Add 1 cup of sorghum and 3 cups of water to a pot on the stove. Bring it to a boil, and then reduce to a simmer. Cover, and cook for 50 minutes.

ONCE UPON A PESTO

Mealie Casserole

MADE WITH CORN PESTO

MAKES 6 TO 8 SERVINGS

TELLTALE and TIME

INTERMEDIATE, 2 HOURS

Once Upon a Pesto

A less finely ground cousin of *mealie pap* is *samp*. It's used in what is said to be Nelson Mandela's favorite recipe, *umngqusho*. This dish of *samp* and cowpeas is a tradition among the people in the Eastern Cape Province of South Africa.

JESSICA PAHOLSKY

South African *mealie pap*, or sometimes called *mealie-meal*, is a porridge similar to polenta or grits. It's coarsely ground maize that's cooked on the stovetop. Many people in South Africa eat it for breakfast with sugar and milk or with syrup and butter. It can also be made savory.

INGREDIENTS

8 cups water

3 1/4 cups yellow cornmeal

1/2 cup Corn Pesto

2 15-ounce cans chopped tomato

4 cups chopped cabbage (1/2 medium head)

3 cups sliced portobello mushrooms (8 ounces)

DIRECTIONS

1. In a large saucepan over low heat, combine the water and cornmeal. Stirring constantly, cook for 10 minutes.

2. Add the Corn Pesto, and stir until incorporated. Remove from the heat.

3. Pour half of the cornmeal mixture into a greased 9-by-13-inch baking dish. Smooth with a spatula and let cool. Then chill in the refrigerator for 30 minutes.

4. Leave the remaining half of the cornmeal mixture at room temperature.

5. Heat oven to 350° F.

6. Meanwhile, in another large saucepan, combine the chopped tomato, cabbage, and portobello mushrooms. Cover and cook for 20 minutes, stirring every 5 minutes.

7. Transfer the chopped tomato mixture to the baking dish atop the chilled first layer of the cornmeal mixture. Smooth the sauce layer with a spatula.

8. Pour the remaining half of the cornmeal mixture atop the sauce layer, warming to liquify if necessary. Smooth with a spatula.

9. Bake for 40 minutes, or until the crust begins to turn golden brown.

10. Let cool for 10 minutes before serving.

Just Right

Traditional *mealie pap* is made with milled white maize. If your local store or market carries it, use white cornmeal instead of yellow cornmeal in this recipe.

ONCE UPON A PESTO

CHAPTER 38: AUSTRALIA
Macadamia Pesto
INSPIRED BY AUSTRALIA

FOLK *or* FAIRY — SAVORY

MAKES 1 CUP

TELLTALE *and* TIME — BEGINNER — 2 MINUTES

JESSICA PAHOLSKY

Australia is one of the world's leading producers of macadamia nuts, which are native to different areas of this country. These buttery nuts got their name from John Macadam, the Scottish-Australian chemist who studied them. It takes macadamia trees seven to ten years until they begin producing nuts, and harvesting them is usually done by hand. Also, macadamia nuts' shells are among the hardest to crack.

INGREDIENTS

1/3 cup shelled unsalted macadamia nuts

1 cup chopped fresh chives

2 cups watercress

1 garlic clove, peeled

1/2 cup shredded cheddar cheese

1/4 cup olive oil

DIRECTIONS

1. Combine all of the ingredients in a food processor. Blend until the desired consistency forms.

2. If using a mortar and pestle, crush the macadamia nuts until smooth. Add the chives, watercress, and garlic. Mash until incorporated. Add the cheddar cheese and olive oil. Mash until the desired consistency forms.

3. Store pesto in an airtight container or jar in the refrigerator for up to one week. Use throughout the week in the next two recipes. Pesto can last in an airtight container in the freezer for up to six months.

Once Upon a Pesto

Australia doesn't quite dominate the food world like other nations, but an important contribution the country made was the macadamia nut. It was discovered by British colonists in Queensland, Australia in 1857.

Kanga-Root Roasted Vegetables

MADE WITH MACADAMIA PESTO

MAKES 6 TO 8 SERVINGS

TELLTALE *and* TIME

INTERMEDIATE, 45 MINUTES

JESSICA PAHOLSKY

Kangaroo is the national animal of Australia, where kangaroo meat is served in many restaurants. However, kangaroo meat is not as widely available as expected, and it's even less common outside of Australia. On the other hand, various vegetables grow well in the temperate regions of the country.

INGREDIENTS

- 1 cup peeled and chopped carrots
- 1 cup peeled and chopped red beets
- 1 cup peeled and chopped golden beets, if available (or 2 cups red beets)
- 1 cup peeled and chopped turnips
- 1 cup chopped onion
- 2 tablespoons olive oil
- 1/4 teaspoon salt
- 1/8 teaspoon pepper
- 1/2 cup Macadamia Pesto
- 1/2 cup dried Zante currants

DIRECTIONS

1. Heat oven to 450° F.
2. In a large mixing bowl, combine the carrots, red beets, turnips, onion, olive oil, salt, and pepper. Toss to coat.
3. Grease a large baking pan. Transfer the vegetables to the pan.
4. Bake for 30 minutes.
5. Let cool for 5 minutes.
6. Gently toss the vegetables with the Macadamia Pesto and Zante currants until incorporated, and serve.

Once Upon a Pesto

Burgers in Australia are often topped with a slice of pickled beetroot, which is one popular vegetable grown there in the spring. Other major vegetable crops include carrots, potatoes, onions, broccoli, cauliflower, and lettuce.

Just Right

Lightly splash the vegetables with a vinegar like apple cider vinegar, along with the olive oil, salt, and pepper. The vinegar's acid will cook off but add even more flavor to the vegetables.

ANZAC Biscuits

MADE WITH MACADAMIA PESTO

MAKES 12 SERVINGS

TELLTALE and TIME
INTERMEDIATE, 40 MINUTES

Once Upon a Pesto

After hearing that their husbands weren't enjoying their food rations, wives of ANZAC soldiers added oats to their biscuit recipe to help soften the biscuits they baked and then sent overseas.

JESSICA PAHOLSKY

ANZAC stands for the Australian and New Zealand Army Corps, which operated during World War I. While overseas in Europe, ANZAC soldiers received care packages that included sweet biscuits baked by their wives back home. Made without eggs, these biscuits could sustain a longer shelf life.

INGREDIENTS

1 cup flour

1 cup oats

3/4 cup unsweetened desiccated coconut

1/4 cup stick butter

1/4 cup Macadamia Pesto

1 teaspoon baking soda

2 tablespoons plus 1/3 cup hot water

1/2 cup shredded cheddar cheese

DIRECTIONS

1. Heat oven to 225° F.
2. In a large mixing bowl, combine the flour, oats, and coconut.
3. Melt the butter in a small pan over medium heat. Add the Macadamia Pesto and stir just until incorporated. Remove from the heat.
4. In a small dish or cup, combine the baking soda and 2 tablespoons of hot water. Stir until dissolved. Add the baking soda mixture to the butter mixture, and stir.
5. Add the baking soda and butter mixture to the flour mixture. Then add the remaining hot water, and stir until a dough forms.
6. Grease a large baking pan.
7. Roll 1 tablespoon of the dough into a ball. Place the dough ball onto the baking pan. Repeat this process of forming and placing dough balls on the pan, spacing the dough balls at least 1 inch apart from the edge of the pan and each other, until all of the dough has been used.
8. Top each dough ball with a pinch of cheddar cheese.
9. Bake for 25 minutes.
10. Transfer the biscuits to a wire cooling rack, and let cool for at least 5 minutes before serving.

Just Right

A perfectly chewy biscuit is ideal. But, if you prefer a crisper version, increase the temperature to 350° F, and bake for 15 to 18 minutes.

CHAPTER 39: NEW ZEALAND
Eggplant Pesto
INSPIRED BY NEW ZEALAND

FOLK or FAIRY — DAIRY-FREE, SAVORY

MAKES 2 CUPS

TELLTALE and TIME — BEGINNER, 2 MINUTES

JESSICA PAHOLSKY

In New Zealand and other English-speaking nations, eggplant is also known as aubergine. During the 18th century, Europeans named this oblong purple vegetable eggplant because it grew in hues of yellow and white, and it was about the size of a goose egg.

INGREDIENTS

1/4 cup shelled raw cashews

3 cups cubed eggplant, cooked in 1 tablespoon olive oil for 10 minutes

1/4 cup chopped pitted green olives

1/4 cup fresh sage

2 tablespoons olive oil

DIRECTIONS

1. Combine all of the ingredients in a food processor. Blend until the desired consistency forms.

2. If using a mortar and pestle, crush the cashews until a fine crumb forms. Add the eggplant and olives, and mash until smooth. Mix in the sage and olive oil. Mash until the desired consistency forms.

3. Store pesto in an airtight container or jar in the refrigerator for up to one week. Use throughout the week in the next two recipes. Pesto can last in an airtight container in the freezer for up to six months.

Once Upon a Pesto

Eggplant is believed to have originated in India, where it still grows wild. As international trade routes opened over the centuries, this vegetable was introduced to Europe and other parts of the world.

Afghan Biscuits

MADE WITH EGGPLANT PESTO

MAKES 24 BISCUITS

TELLTALE and TIME
INTERMEDIATE, 50 MINUTES

Once Upon a Pesto

Contrary to the origin the name of these cookies indicates, Afghan biscuits are native to New Zealand. In fact, the treat appeared multiple times in the 1940 edition of the institutional cookbook of New Zealand, *The Sure to Rise Cookery Book* by TJ Edmonds.

JESSICA PAHOLSKY

Made in New Zealand, Afghan biscuits are bite-sized, leavening-free cookies traditionally made with cornflakes and cocoa powder, topped with icing, and garnished with half of a nut. There are various meanings behind the use of the word Afghan, too. Two of those include a person from Afghanistan and a knitted blanket.

INGREDIENTS

3/4 cup butter, at room temperature

1/2 cup sugar

1 3/4 cup all-purpose flour

6 tablespoons Eggplant Pesto

1 1/2 cups unsweetened corn flakes

For the icing:

1/4 cup unsalted butter, at room temperature

2 ounces cream cheese

1 cup powdered sugar

8 pitted kalamata olives, finely chopped

24 cashew halves

DIRECTIONS

1. Heat oven to 350° F.
2. To make the biscuit dough, in a large mixing bowl, combine the butter and sugar. Cream until fluffy.
3. Mix in the flour and Eggplant Pesto. Stir until incorporated.
4. Gently fold the corn flakes into the batter.
5. Prepare a cookie sheet with greased aluminum foil.
6. Scoop 1 tablespoon of the batter at a time, roll it into a ball, and then gently flatten it. Place it on the prepared cookie sheet.
7. Repeat step 6, leaving 1 inch between each biscuit, until all of the batter is used.
8. Bake for 12 minutes, or until golden brown on the edges.
9. Let cool on a wire rack for at least 20 minutes after baking.
10. Meanwhile, prepare the icing by beating together the butter and cream cheese.
11. Add the powdered sugar and mix until incorporated.
12. Stir in the olives.
13. Spoon 1 to 2 teaspoons of the icing onto each cooled biscuit.
14. Top each biscuit with a cashew half.
15. Serve, or store in an airtight container in the refrigerator for up to 1 week.

Just Right

The corn flakes add a unique crispness to these soft biscuits. Feel free to experiment with other similar cereal types.

Breakfast Sausages

MADE WITH EGGPLANT PESTO

MAKES 12 SAUSAGE PATTIES

TELLTALE and TIME

INTERMEDIATE, 40 MINUTES

JESSICA PAHOLSKY

In New Zealand, sausage sizzles are a popular community event where sausages are grilled or barbecued and then served in sliced bread or on a hot dog roll. The event can be free or used as a fundraiser for a local community organization like public schools.

INGREDIENTS

3 pounds ground turkey

1 cup Eggplant Pesto

1 teaspoon ground black pepper

1/2 teaspoon salt

DIRECTIONS

1. In a large mixing bowl, combine all of the ingredients. Mix until incorporated.

2. Refrigerate for 15 minutes.

3. Divide the mixture into 12 portions, and shape each portion into a patty about 3/4 inch thick.

4. Cook, or freeze the sausage patties between sheets of wax paper for up to 6 months and then thaw in the refrigerator overnight when ready to use.

5. In a large pan over medium heat, cook the sausage patties for 4 to 5 minutes per side, working in batches as needed.

6. Transfer the cooked sausage patties to a paper towel-lined plate.

7. Serve with a side of hash browns or on a toasted English muffin.

Once Upon a Pesto

People in New Zealand call sausages bangers, snarlers, or barbecue fodder.

Just Right

The most commonly used meat at a sausage sizzle is pork or beef. Simply replace the ground turkey in this recipe with 3 pounds of your preferred ground meat.

CHAPTER 40: FIJI
Pickle Pesto

INSPIRED BY FIJI

FOLK or FAIRY — DAIRY-FREE, SAVORY

MAKES 1¼ CUPS

TELLTALE and TIME — BEGINNER, 2 MINUTES

JESSICA PAHOLSKY

In Fiji, pickling is a valuable process in the context of marriage. The people native to Fiji pickle their foods in banana-leaf-lined pits. These pits can then provide a source of food in case of severe storms. But, perhaps more importantly, if well-stocked, these pits help indicate if a man is able to provide for his future wife.

INGREDIENTS

1/4 cup shelled macadamia nuts

1 3/4 cups chopped whole dill pickles

1 cup chopped fresh curly-leaf parsley

1/4 cup chopped fresh chives

1 teaspoon dill pickle juice

1/4 teaspoon paprika

1/4 teaspoon ground mustard seed

DIRECTIONS

1. Combine all of the ingredients in a food processor. Blend until the desired consistency forms.

2. If using a mortar and pestle, crush the macadamia nuts until a fine crumb forms. Add the pickles, parsley, and chives, and mash until fairly smooth. Mix in the remaining ingredients. Mash until the desired consistency forms.

3. Store pesto in an airtight container or jar in the refrigerator for up to one week. Use throughout the week in the next two recipes. Pesto can last in an airtight container in the freezer for up to six months.

Once Upon a Pesto

The process of pickling foods is believed to have begun as far back in time as 2400 BC. What about actual pickles? Cucumbers were first pickled several centuries later in Western Asia.

ONCE UPON A PESTO

Bloody Mary

MADE WITH PICKLE PESTO

MAKES 4 SERVINGS

TELLTALE *and* TIME

BEGINNER, 10 MINUTES

JESSICA PAHOLSKY

Tomato juice is a key ingredient in Bloody Mary, which possibly got its name as a reference to England during the 16th century. Tomatoes are also one of the most common vegetables grown in Fiji. In fact, tomatoes can grow year round on these islands. However, Fiji still imports a significant amount of tomatoes and other produce from New Zealand and Australia to support the demand among its people.

INGREDIENTS

4 cups tomato juice

1 cup vodka

1 tablespoon Worcestershire sauce

2 teaspoons Tabasco sauce

1/2 cup Pickle Pesto

paprika and salt

1 cup crushed or small ice cubes

DIRECTIONS

1. Combine the tomato juice, vodka, Worcestershire sauce, Tabasco sauce, and Pickle Pesto in a blender. Blend until smooth.

2. Mix the paprika and salt in a one-to-one ratio on a small, flat plate. Lightly wet with water or fresh lemon juice the rims of four serving glasses, such as pint-sized mason jars. Then dip each glass rim in the paprika-salt mixture.

3. Divide the ice among the four glasses.

4. Divide the tomato juice mixture among the four glasses, and serve.

Once Upon a Pesto

The drink Bloody Mary was created during the 1920s in Paris, France. It isn't common in Fiji. On the other hand, Fiji's national drink, kava, is a beverage made from mixing the powdered root of a pepper plant with water.

Just Right

Garnish your Bloody Mary glasses with a pickle slice, piece of celery, stuffed olive, or lemon wedge, if desired.

Mack and Cheese

MADE WITH PICKLE PESTO

MAKES 4 TO 5 SERVINGS

TELLTALE *and* TIME

INTERMEDIATE, 45 MINUTES

Jessica Paholsky

Fiji is a nation made up of about 330 different islands. As a South Pacific archipelago, fish is readily available to Fijian residents and visitors. One type of fish common in Fiji is mackerel, which is often sold in the canned foods section of most supermarkets.

INGREDIENTS

4 tablespoons butter

1/4 cup flour

1 cup milk

1/2 cup Pickle Pesto

4 ounces cream cheese

1 1/2 cups shredded four-cheese blend cheese

3 4-ounce cans mackerel, broken into pieces

8 ounces pasta (such as radiatore, elbows, or shells), cooked and drained

1/2 cup plain panko bread crumbs

DIRECTIONS

1. Heat oven to 350° F.
2. In a medium saucepan, melt the butter over medium-low heat.
3. Add the flour, whisking until combined and smooth.
4. Add the milk and Pickle Pesto, stirring until incorporated.
5. Add the cream cheese and 1 cup of the four-cheese blend.
6. Stir until melted and smooth.
7. Add the mackerel and pasta.
8. Gently stir until coated.
9. Transfer to a lightly oiled 8-inch cast iron pan.
10. Sprinkle the remaining four-blend cheese and the panko bread crumbs on top.
11. Bake for 25 minutes, or until the crust is lightly browned.
12. Let cool for 5 minutes before serving.

Once Upon a Pesto

Fishing in Fiji varies seasonally. Mahi mahi is a popular deepwater fish found and eaten there. Another very large catch is yellowfin tuna.

Just Right

If you prefer a more classic take on this recipe, replace the 10 ounces of mackerel with an equivalent amount of canned tuna. Or for a fish-free option, replace the mackerel with 1 cup of thawed frozen peas.

Acknowledgments

Once upon a time, I set a goal to publish a cookbook. That was in 2016, when I began my job as a video producer at a publishing company. Today, here I am: a published cookbook author. It couldn't have happened without the support, encouragement, and wisdom from several people who I'd like to acknowledge. Their round-the-clock advice, compliments, and personal networks helped make this book, as well as my website and social media presence, possible.

I think the biggest lesson I've learned in this six-year journey is that persistence and connections do pay off. What seemed like a mountain to climb with speed bumps and jagged edges all along the way became more like a long Sunday drive with the windows rolled down, ocean air blowing through my hair, and my favorite tunes on the radio. I see now how every challenge is beautiful in its own way. And like they say, "Rome wasn't built in a day." While *Once Upon a Pesto* is in no way interchangeable with this Italian capital city, they do share some things in common—the history of pesto.

Developing my pesto recipes, creating written and visual content, and unifying it all through a branded voice and personality has and will continue to bring me joy. But I also receive so much joy through the people I meet, the relationships I build, and the affirmation that what I present through *Once Upon a Pesto* helps educate, entertain, and inspire others around the globe.

If you believe in yourself, you can do anything, even change the world. For a realist like myself, that may be a stretch. But if others believe in you—and acknowledge that continually—there's a fire that burns passion and dedication inside you. I'd like to thank every person who does exactly that for me. I don't have the space to list every single person, so here's to those contacts who have played small, albeit significant, roles in my cookbook publishing journey.

More specifically, I want to thank my immediate family. With familial relationships that are positive and open to my many and unique passions, I have had the ability to chase my dreams. To my dad, Tom: Thank you for tuning into every Instagram live video I host, for promoting my work in the local community through Rotary as well as other local organizations and businesses, and for always staying up to date on where my name is being published and promoted through the media. To my mom, Carolyn, and step-dad, Dave: Thank you for laying a culinary foundation from which I could grow practically and creatively, for promoting a homestead lifestyle of gardening and preserving foods, and for spearheading my international travel bug with a trip to Mexico in 2011. To my sister, Andrea: Thank you for gifting me a copy of *The Flavor Bible: The Essential Guide to Culinary Creativity,* which served as the biggest single source of information and inspiration for my recipe development. To my grandparents, aunts, uncles, and cousins: Thank you for continually following me on this journey, for expressing excitement with every step, and, to my grandparents, for watching over me from heaven as this dream became a reality.

I've also been blessed with friendships all over the map. While some friendships come and go, there are several that have endured geographic moves, new jobs, and new residences to be constant supportive voices and ears. To best capture these connections, I'll do so by groups. To my current and former colleagues, members of my current and former churches, friends at my current and former gyms, and friends and connections established during grade school and college: Thank you for discovering my pesto passion through social media, the news, or in-person conversations and actively following up as the process of publishing progressed. Some have joked that they didn't know I ever had such a side hobby, and many have gotten to partake in pesto sampling. Either or both of these discoveries gripped them into learning more about *Once Upon a Pesto* and my goals. And to all residents of my hometown and birth town: Thank you for giving me all the more reason to be proud of my roots and for reaching out whenever you saw my name or brand in a headline.

I like to think of *Once Upon a Pesto* as a hybrid approach to the industries of my first two full-time jobs: the travel industry and the publishing industry. These significant life influences and experiences advanced my knowledge and ignited my passions to create something completely new. Early in my college experience, I told many people my goal was to be a photographer for *National Geographic*. Well, when you think of the travel and publishing industries, you can end up with a name like *National Geographic* or you can think of them separately as I experienced them. In the travel industry, my two years at Travel For Teens opened my eyes to the impact and value of international travel among youth. It took me to three continents over two summers—most countries for the very first time. In the publishing industry, my time at Rodale, Inc. led to professional connections, growth, and conclusions that couldn't be taught elsewhere. With food, fitness, and wellness as the brand's key subjects, I was able to establish my pesto niche, make a few of my own recipes in a real test kitchen, and seek advice from published food writers and editors. Thank you to everyone from these organizations who played a part in my journey and for maintaining our connections despite the physical distances that came with my next opportunities.

If this text were being delivered verbally, this is probably the part where I would get most choked up. I can't speak from direct experience, but I would venture to say most teachers and professors only have a handful of students who maintain contact with them over the years. I'm beyond fortunate to say that I am one of those students with both teachers from Littlestown Area School District and professors at Penn State University. These selfless educators have gone above and beyond their roles to nurture me in my younger years, teach me what learning is all about, inspire me to set and accomplish my goals, and offer mentorship whenever I reach out. To my elementary school and, later, high school art and photography teacher, Mrs. Becker: You are probably the only one who has seen me through my "most shy" years, besides my parents. Every step of the way, you were there to teach me creativity and inspire me to pursue my passion for art. Thank you for continuing to love my love for pesto and even make some of my pesto recipes. To my college professors, Randy Ploog and Patrick Tunno: Your impact on my life cannot be appropriately articulated. From enabling my study abroad experiences—Randy—and showing me how Italian and other languages can be used after academic life—Prof. Tunno—you both have something to take credit for in this published book.

Though faculty in different departments at Penn State, you both share in common Italian travel and genuine interest in the success of your students. Lastly, I would like to dedicate *Once Upon a Pesto* in memory of my photojournalism professor and college thesis advisor, Curt Chandler. Thank you, Curt, for inspiring my professional and personal storytelling experiences to grow more rich every day. Your wisdom and personal life stories have impacted more people than you'll ever know. May your legacy of kindness and patience live on through generations to come.

Finally and most indisputably, I would like to express great appreciation to this book's designer and publisher. To the very talented graphic artist, Rachel Loughlin: Your vision and execution on every page, in every small detail has brought to life the time I've poured into this project. The subtleties of your work more than matched what I wanted this book to become. I am in awe of how you applied the concept of *Once Upon a Pesto*, with its globalness and sensory experience, in layouts that are rich in color and imagery. And to Usher Morgan and the Library Tales Publishing team: My gratitude and sense of fulfillment is owed to you. From our first phone call to the knowledge and quality you've been committed to throughout the publishing process, it has been a wonderful journey. I deeply appreciate your mission, belief in the power of books, and dedication to timeless storytelling. And I am so glad *Once Upon a Pesto* will bear the Library Tales name. Thank you sincerely for all your work in transforming this cookbook into a format we can share with curious minds around the world.

Jessica Paholsky

INDEX

A

Asparagus
- Asparagus Pesto (*Peru*) — 58

B

Bacon
- Bacon Monkey Bread (*Canada*) — 48

Bamboo Shoots
- Bamboo Shoots Salad (*Myanmar*) — 196

Banana
- Banana Pesto (*Uganda*) — 226

Barley
- Barley Minestrone (*Switzerland*) — 106

Beans and Legumes
- Spiced Lentils (*Ethiopia*) — 224
- Succotash (*Southern United States*) — 32
- Tamale Cups (*Mayan*) — 24

Beef
- Roast Beef Pinwheels (*Iran*) — 148
- Salisbury Steak (*Mayan*) — 26

Beets
- Beet Brownies (*Belgium*) — 92

Biscuits
- Afghan Biscuits (*New Zealand*) — 252
- ANZAC Biscuits (*Australia*) — 248

Bloody Mary
- Bloody Mary (*Fiji*) — 258

BLT
- French Toast BLT (*France*) — 88

Bowls
- Hummus Bowl (*Greece*) — 124

Breads
- Bacon Monkey Bread (*Canada*) — 48
- Naan Bread (*Iran*) — 150
- Plantain Bread (*Nigeria*) — 210
- Walnut Swirl Bread (*Croatia*) — 118

Breakfast
- Breakfast Sausages (*New Zealand*) — 254

Broccoli
- Broccoli Pesto (*France*) — 84

Brownies
- Beet Brownies (*Belgium*) — 92

Brussels Sprouts
- Brussels Sprouts Gratin (*Belgium*) — 94

Burgers
- Millet Burgers (*Korea*) — 174

C

Cabbage (Red)
- Red Cabbage Pesto (*Spain*) — 78

Capers
- Caper Pesto (*Cyprus*) — 126

Cantaloupe
- Cantaloupe Pesto (*Armenia*) — 140

Candy/Confectionery
- Churchkhela (*Georgia*) — 136
- Coconut Barfi (*India*) — 156
- Marshmallows (*Russia*) — 162

Carrot
- Carrot Pesto (*India*) — 152

Cassava
- Cassava Muffins (*Uganda*) — 230
- Cassava Pesto (*Mozambique*) — 232

Casseroles
- Mealie Casserole *(South Africa)* — 242

Cauliflower
- Stir-Fried Cauliflower Rice *(China)* — 166

Celery
- Celery Pesto *(Korea)* — 170

Cherry
- Cherry Pesto *(Russia)* — 158

Chia Seeds
- Mushroom and Chia Pesto *(Mayan)* — 22

Chicken
- Chicken Dumplings *(China)* — 168
- Chicken Pot Pie Crêpes *(France)* — 86
- Spiced Chicken *(Uganda)* — 228
- Yellow Chicken Curry *(Thailand)* — 192

Chili
- Chili *(Chile)* — 66

Coconut
- Coconut Barfi *(India)* — 156

Coffee
- Coffee Flan *(Brazil)* — 74

Coleslaw
- Caribbean Coleslaw *(Puerto Rico)* — 54

Collard Greens
- Collard Greens Pesto *(Southern United States)* — 28

Corn
- Corn Pesto *(South Africa)* — 238
- Street Corn *(Peru)* — 62
- Succotash *(Southern United States)* — 32

Couscous
- Couscous Salad *(Morocco)* — 204

Cranberry
- Cranberry Nausamp *(Native American)* — 20

Crêpes
- Chicken Pot Pie Crêpes *(France)* — 86

Curry
- Yellow Chicken Curry *(Thailand)* — 192

D

Daikon
- Daikon Pesto *(Japan)* — 176

Deviled Eggs
- Deviled Eggs *(Southern United States)* — 30

Dips
- Feta Dip *(Cyprus)* — 128
- Stone Fruit Salsa *(Croatia)* — 116

Donuts
- Sopaipillas *(Chile)* — 68

Drinks
- Bloody Mary *(Fiji)* — 258
- Piña Colada *(Puerto Rico)* — 56
- Rum Milkshake *(Canada)* — 50

Dumplings
- Chicken Dumplings *(China)* — 168

E

Edamame
- Edamame *(Japan)* — 180

Eggplant
- Eggplant Parmesan Lasagna Stacks *(Italy)* — 112
- Eggplant Pesto *(New Zealand)* — 250
- Eggplant Rolls *(Georgia)* — 134

ONCE UPON A PESTO

Eggs
    Deviled Eggs   30
    (Southern United States)
    Korean Egg Roll *(Korea)*   172
    Spanish Tortilla *(Spain)*   82
Endive
    Endive Pesto *(Belgium)*   90

F
Feta
    Feta Dip *(Cyprus)*   128
Fish
    Swedish Tuna Balls *(Sweden)*   100
Flan
    Coffee Flan *(Brazil)*   74
French Toast
    French Toast BLT *(France)*   88
Fruit Leather *(Armenia)*   142

G
Galette
    Leek Galette *(Switzerland)*   104
Gratin
    Brussels Sprouts Gratin *(Belgium)*   94
Grapes
    Grape Pesto *(Georgia)*   132
Green Beans
    Green Bean Pesto *(New York)*   40

H
Hummus
    Hummus Bowl *(Greece)*   124

K
Kale
    Kale Salad *(Midwest United States)*   36
Kebabs
    Sheftalia *(Cyprus)*   130

L
Lamb
    Lamb with Candied Fruit *(Morocco)*   206
Leek
    Leek Galette *(Switzerland)*   104
Lemon
    Lemon Pesto *(Myanmar)*   194
Lemongrass
    Lemongrass Pesto *(Malaysia)*   182
Lentils
    Spiced Lentils *(Ethiopia)*   224
Lima Beans
    Succotash *(Southern United States)*   32

M
Macadamia Nuts
    Macadamia Pesto *(Australia)*   244
Mac and Cheese
    Mack and Cheese *(Fiji)*   260
    Mac 'N Cheese *(Egypt)*   218
Mackerel
    Mack and Cheese *(Fiji)*   260
Mango
    Mango Pesto *(Thailand)*   188
Maple Syrup
    Maple Syrup Pesto *(Canada)*   46
Marshmallows
    Marshmallows *(Russia)*   162

Meatloaf
    Stuffed Turkey Meatloaf *(Native American)* ... 18
Meats
    Citrus Ribs *(Brazil)* ... 72
    Lamb with Candied Fruit *(Morocco)* ... 206
    Salisbury Steak *(Mayan)* ... 26
    Sheftalia *(Cyprus)* ... 130
    Spiced Chicken *(Uganda)* ... 228
    Stuffed Turkey Meatloaf *(Native American)* ... 18
    Yellow Chicken Curry *(Thailand)* ... 192
Melons
    Melon Gazpacho *(Spain)* ... 80
Millet
    Millet Burgers *(Korea)* ... 174
Minestrone
    Barley Minestrone *(Switzerland)* ... 106
Muffins
    Cassava Muffins *(Uganda)* ... 230
Mushrooms
    Mushroom and Chia Pesto *(Mayan)* ... 22

O

Oats
    Oatmeal Bars *(Russia)* ... 160
Octopus
    Watermelon Ceviche *(Mozambique)* ... 236
Okra
    Okra Pesto *(Ethiopia)* ... 220
Olives
    Olive Pesto *(Egypt)* ... 214

Onions
    Onion Pesto *(Iran)* ... 146
Orzo
    Orzo Pilaf *(Armenia)* ... 144

P

Parsley
    Parsley Pesto *(Greece)* ... 120
Passion Fruit
    Passion Fruit Pesto *(Puerto Rico)* ... 52
Pasta
    Crispy Gnocchi *(Midwest United States)* ... 38
    Couscous Salad *(Morocco)* ... 204
    Mack and Cheese *(Fiji)* ... 260
    Mac 'N Cheese *(Egypt)* ... 218
    Orzo Pilaf *(Armenia)* ... 144
Pastries
    Kuih Puffs *(Malaysia)* ... 184
    Sweet Buns *(Sweden)* ... 98
Peanuts
    Peanut Stew *(Nigeria)* ... 212
Pecans
    Pecan Pesto *(Midwest United States)* ... 34
Peppers (Bell)
    Red Pepper Salad *(Thailand)* ... 190
    Risotto-Stuffed Peppers *(Italy)* ... 110
Pickles
    Pickle Pesto *(Fiji)* ... 256
Pilafs
    Orzo Pilaf *(Armenia)* ... 144
    Sorghum Pilaf *(South Africa)* ... 240
Pizza
    Reuben Pizza *(New York)* ... 42

Plantains
    Plantain Bread *(Nigeria)* — 210

Popcorn
    Stovetop Popcorn *(Ethiopia)* — 222

Porridge
    Cranberry Nausamp *(Native American)* — 20

Puffs
    Kuih Puffs *(Malaysia)* — 184

Pineapple
    Piña Colada *(Puerto Rico)* — 56
    Pineapple Pesto *(Brazil)* — 70

Plum
    Plum Pesto *(Croatia)* — 114

Pudding
    Tapioca Pudding *(Myanmar)* — 198

Pumpkin
    Pumpkin Pesto *(Native American)* — 16

Q

Quinoa
    Quinoa Soup *(Peru)* — 60

R

Ramen
    Ramen Salad *(India)* — 154

Rhubarb
    Rhubarb Pesto *(Chile)* — 64

Ribs
    Citrus Ribs *(Brazil)* — 72

Rice
    Dolmades *(Greece)* — 122
    Risotto-Stuffed Peppers *(Italy)* — 110
    Stir-Fried Cauliflower Rice *(China)* — 166
    Sushi Stack *(Japan)* — 178

Risotto
    Risotto-Stuffed Peppers *(Italy)* — 110

Roast Beef
    Roast Beef Pinwheels *(Iran)* — 148

Roasted Vegetables
    Kanga-Root Roasted Vegetables *(Australia)* — 246

Rum
    Rum Milkshake *(Canada)* — 50

Rutabaga
    Rutabaga Pesto *(Sweden)* — 96

S

Salads
    Bamboo Shoots Salad *(Myanmar)* — 196
    Chef Salad *(New York)* — 44
    Couscous Salad *(Morocco)* — 204
    Hummus Bowl *(Greece)* — 124
    Kale Salad *(Midwest United States)* — 36
    Mediterranean Salad *(Egypt)* — 216
    Ramen Salad *(India)* — 154

Salsa
    Stone Fruit Salsa *(Croatia)* — 116

Sandwiches
    French Toast BLT *(France)* — 88
    Reuben Pizza *(New York)* — 42

Satay
    Shrimp Satay *(Malaysia)* — 186

Sausage
    Breakfast Sausages *(New Zealand)*   254
Shrimp
    Shrimp Satay *(Malaysia)*   186
Sorghum
    Sorghum Pilaf *(South Africa)*   240
Soups
    Chili *(Chile)*   66
    Melon Gazpacho *(Spain)*   80
    Peanut Stew *(Nigeria)*   212
Quinoa Soup *(Peru)*
Spices
    Spices Pesto *(Morocco)*   202
Spinach
    Spinach Pesto *(China)*   164
Steak
    Salisbury Steak *(Mayan)*   26
Stews
    Peanut Stew *(Nigeria)*   212
Stir Fries
    Stir-Fried Cauliflower Rice *(China)*   166
Sushi
    Sushi Stack *(Japan)*   178
Swiss Chard
    Swiss Chard Pesto *(Switzerland)*   102

T

Tamales
    Tamale Cups *(Mayan)*   24
Tapioca
    Tapioca Pudding *(Myanmar)*   198
Tomato
    Tomato Cobbler *(Mozambique)*   234
Tuna
    Swedish Tuna Balls *(Sweden)*   100
Turkey
    Stuffed Turkey Meatloaf *(Native American)*   18

V

Vegetables
    Kanga-Root Roasted Vegetables *(Australia)*   246

W

Walnuts
    Walnut Swirl Bread *(Croatia)*   118
Wraps
    Roast Beef Pinwheels *(Iran)*   148
Watermelon
    Watermelon Ceviche *(Mozambique)*   236

Y

Yams
    Yam Pesto *(Nigeria)*   208

Z

Zucchini
    Zucchini Pesto *(Italy)*   108

INDEX BY CATEGORY

BY DISHES

APPETIZERS

Deviled Eggs *(Southern United States)*	30
Dolmades *(Greece)*	122
Edamame *(Japan)*	180
Eggplant Rolls *(Georgia)*	134
Feta Dip *(Cyprus)*	128
Leek Galette *(Switzerland)*	104
Roast Beef Pinwheels *(Iran)*	148
Stone Fruit Salsa *(Croatia)*	116
Watermelon Ceviche *(Mozambique)*	236

BEEF AND OTHER MEATS

Citrus Ribs *(Brazil)*	72
Lamb with Candied Fruit *(Morocco)*	206
Salisbury Steak *(Mayan)*	26
Sheftalia *(Cyprus)*	130

BREAKFASTS AND BRUNCHES

Breakfast Sausages *(New Zealand)*	254
Chicken Pot Pie Crêpes *(France)*	86
Cranberry Nausamp *(Native American)*	20
Korean Egg Roll *(Korea)*	172
Oatmeal Bars *(Russia)*	160
Spanish Tortilla *(Spain)*	82
Tomato Cobbler *(Mozambique)*	234

CHICKEN AND POULTRY

Chicken Dumplings *(China)*	168
Spiced Chicken *(Uganda)*	228
Stuffed Turkey Meatloaf *(Native American)*	18
Yellow Chicken Curry *(Thailand)*	192

DESSERTS AND SNACKS

Afghan Biscuits *(New Zealand)*	252
ANZAC Biscuits *(Australia)*	248
Bacon Monkey Bread *(Canada)*	48
Beet Brownies *(Belgium)*	92
Cassava Muffins *(Uganda)*	230
Churchkhela *(Georgia)*	136
Coconut Barfi *(India)*	156
Coffee Flan *(Brazil)*	74
Fruit Leather *(Armenia)*	142
Kuih Puffs *(Malaysia)*	184
Marshmallows *(Russia)*	162
Plantain Bread *(Nigeria)*	210
Sopaipillas *(Chile)*	68
Stovetop Popcorn *(Ethiopia)*	222
Sweet Buns *(Sweden)*	98
Tapioca Pudding *(Myanmar)*	198
Walnut Swirl Bread *(Croatia)*	118

DRINKS

Bloody Mary *(Fiji)*	258
Piña Colada *(Puerto Rico)*	56
Rum Milkshake *(Canada)*	50

FISH AND SEAFOOD

Shrimp Satay *(Malaysia)*	186
Swedish Tuna Balls *(Sweden)*	100

MAIN COURSES

Chicken Dumplings *(China)*	168
Citrus Ribs *(Brazil)*	72
Crispy Gnocchi *(Midwest United States)*	38
Eggplant Parmesan Lasagna Stacks *(Italy)*	112
French Toast BLT *(France)*	88
Lamb with Candied Fruit *(Morocco)*	206
Mack and Cheese *(Fiji)*	260
Mealie Casserole *(South Africa)*	242
Millet Burgers *(Korea)*	174
Reuben Pizza *(New York)*	42
Salisbury Steak *(Mayan)*	26
Sheftalia *(Cyprus)*	130
Shrimp Satay *(Malaysia)*	186
Spiced Chicken *(Uganda)*	228
Spiced Lentils *(Ethiopia)*	224
Stuffed Turkey Meatloaf *(Native American)*	18
Sushi Stack *(Japan)*	178
Swedish Tuna Balls *(Sweden)*	100
Tamale Cups *(Mayan)*	24
Yellow Chicken Curry *(Thailand)*	192

MEATLESS MAINS

Eggplant Parmesan Lasagna Stacks *(Italy)*	112
Mack and Cheese *(Fiji)*	260
Mealie Casserole *(South Africa)*	242
Millet Burgers *(Korea)*	174
Spiced Lentils *(Ethiopia)*	224
Sushi Stack *(Japan)*	178
Tamale Cups *(Mayan)*	24

PASTAS AND OTHER ITALIAN DISHES

Crispy Gnocchi *(Midwest United States)*	38
Eggplant Parmesan Lasagna Stacks *(Italy)*	112
Mack and Cheese *(Fiji)*	260
Mac 'N Cheese *(Egypt)*	218
Orzo Pilaf *(Armenia)*	144
Reuben Pizza *(New York)*	42
Risotto-Stuffed Peppers *(Italy)*	110

SALADS

Bamboo Shoots Salad *(Myanmar)*	196
Chef Salad *(New York)*	44
Hummus Bowl *(Greece)*	124
Kale Salad *(Midwest United States)*	36
Mediterranean Salad *(Egypt)*	216
Ramen Salad *(India)*	154
Red Pepper Salad *(Thailand)*	190

SANDWICHES

French Toast BLT *(France)*	88
Millet Burgers *(Korea)*	174

SIDES

Brussels Sprouts Gratin *(Belgium)*	94
Caribbean Coleslaw *(Puerto Rico)*	54

ONCE UPON A PESTO

Couscous Salad *(Morocco)*	204
Kanga-Root Roasted Vegetables *(Australia)*	246
Mac 'N Cheese *(Egypt)*	218
Naan Bread *(Iran)*	150
Orzo Pilaf *(Armenia)*	144
Risotto-Stuffed Peppers *(Italy)*	110
Sorghum Pilaf *(South Africa)*	240
Stir-Fried Cauliflower Rice *(China)*	166
Street Corn *(Peru)*	62
Succotash *(Southern United States)*	32

SOUPS

Barley Minestrone *(Switzerland)*	106
Chili *(Chile)*	66
Melon Gazpacho *(Spain)*	80
Peanut Stew *(Nigeria)*	212
Quinoa Soup *(Peru)*	60

VEGETABLES

Brussels Sprouts Gratin *(Belgium)*	94
Caribbean Coleslaw *(Puerto Rico)*	54
Kanga-Root Roasted Vegetables *(Australia)*	246
Stir-Fried Cauliflower Rice *(China)*	166
Street Corn *(Peru)*	62
Succotash *(Southern United States)*	32

BY PESTO TYPES

DAIRY-FREE PESTOS

Banana Pesto *(Uganda)*	226
Cantaloupe Pesto *(Armenia)*	140
Cassava Pesto *(Mozambique)*	232
Celery Pesto *(Korea)*	170
Collard Greens Pesto *(Southern United States)*	28
Daikon Pesto *(Japan)*	176
Eggplant Pesto *(New Zealand)*	250
Lemongrass Pesto *(Malaysia)*	182
Maple Syrup Pesto *(Canada)*	46
Okra Pesto *(Ethiopia)*	220
Parsley Pesto *(Greece)*	120
Passion Fruit Pesto *(Puerto Rico)*	52
Pickle Pesto *(Fiji)*	256
Pineapple Pesto *(Brazil)*	70
Plum Pesto *(Croatia)*	114
Red Cabbage Pesto *(Spain)*	78
Rhubarb Pesto *(Chile)*	64
Rutabaga Pesto *(Sweden)*	96
Spices Pesto *(Morocco)*	202

NUT-FREE PESTOS

Banana Pesto *(Uganda)*	226
Broccoli Pesto *(France)*	84
Carrot Pesto *(India)*	152

Corn Pesto *(South Africa)*	238
Daikon Pesto *(Japan)*	176
Mushroom and Chia Pesto *(Mayan)*	22
Okra Pesto *(Ethiopia)*	220
Olive Pesto *(Egypt)*	214
Red Cabbage Pesto *(Spain)*	78
Rutabaga Pesto *(Sweden)*	96
Spinach Pesto *(China)*	164

SAVORY PESTOS

Asparagus Pesto *(Peru)*	58
Broccoli Pesto *(France)*	84
Caper Pesto *(Cyprus)*	126
Carrot Pesto *(India)*	152
Cassava Pesto *(Mozambique)*	232
Celery Pesto *(Korea)*	170
Collard Greens Pesto *(Southern United States)*	28
Corn Pesto *(South Africa)*	238
Daikon Pesto *(Japan)*	176
Eggplant Pesto *(New Zealand)*	250
Endive Pesto *(Belgium)*	90
Green Bean Pesto *(New York)*	40
Lemongrass Pesto *(Malaysia)*	182
Macadamia Pesto *(Australia)*	244
Maple Syrup Pesto *(Canada)*	46
Mushroom and Chia Pesto *(Mayan)*	22
Okra Pesto *(Ethiopia)*	220
Olive Pesto *(Egypt)*	214
Onion Pesto *(Iran)*	146
Parsley Pesto *(Greece)*	120
Pecan Pesto *(Midwest United States)*	34
Pickle Pesto *(Fiji)*	256
Pumpkin Pesto *(Native American)*	16
Cabbage Pesto *(Spain)*	78
Rhubarb Pesto *(Chile)*	64
Rutabaga Pesto *(Sweden)*	96
Spices Pesto *(Morocco)*	202
Spinach Pesto *(China)*	164
Swiss Chard Pesto *(Switzerland)*	102
Yam Pesto *(Nigeria)*	208
Zucchini Pesto *(Italy)*	108

SWEET PESTOS

Banana Pesto *(Uganda)*	226
Cantaloupe Pesto *(Armenia)*	140
Cherry Pesto *(Russia)*	158
Grape Pesto *(Georgia)*	132
Lemon Pesto *(Myanmar)*	194
Mango Pesto *(Thailand)*	188
Passion Fruit Pesto *(Puerto Rico)*	52
Pineapple Pesto *(Brazil)*	70
Plum Pesto *(Croatia)*	114

BY COUNTRIES OR CULTURES

Armenia

Cantaloupe Pesto *(Armenia)*	140
Fruit Leather *(Armenia)*	142
Orzo Pilaf *(Armenia)*	144

Australia

ANZAC Biscuits *(Australia)*	248
Kanga-Root Roasted Vegetables *(Australia)*	246
Macadamia Pesto *(Australia)*	244

Belgium

Beet Brownies *(Belgium)*	92
Brussels Sprouts Gratin *(Belgium)*	94
Endive Pesto *(Belgium)*	90

Brazil

Citrus Ribs *(Brazil)*	72
Coffee Flan *(Brazil)*	74
Pineapple Pesto *(Brazil)*	70

Canada

Bacon Monkey Bread *(Canada)*	48
Maple Syrup Pesto *(Canada)*	46
Rum Milkshake *(Canada)*	50

Chile

Chili *(Chile)*	66
Rhubarb Pesto *(Chile)*	64
Sopaipillas *(Chile)*	68

China

Chicken Dumplings *(China)*	168
Spinach Pesto *(China)*	164
Stir-Fried Cauliflower Rice *(China)*	166

Croatia

Plum Pesto *(Croatia)*	114
Stone Fruit Salsa *(Croatia)*	116
Walnut Swirl Bread *(Croatia)*	118

Cyprus

Caper Pesto *(Cyprus)*	126
Feta Dip *(Cyprus)*	128
Sheftalia *(Cyprus)*	130

Egypt

Mac 'N Cheese *(Egypt)*	218
Mediterranean Salad *(Egypt)*	216
Olive Pesto *(Egypt)*	214

Ethiopia

Okra Pesto *(Ethiopia)*	220
Spiced Lentils *(Ethiopia)*	224
Stovetop Popcorn *(Ethiopia)*	222

Fiji

Bloody Mary *(Fiji)*	258
Mack and Cheese *(Fiji)*	260
Pickle Pesto *(Fiji)*	256

France

Broccoli Pesto *(France)*	84
Chicken Pot Pie Crêpes *(France)*	86
French Toast BLT *(France)*	88

Georgia

Churchkhela *(Georgia)*	136
Eggplant Rolls *(Georgia)*	134
Grape Pesto *(Georgia)*	132

Greece

Dolmades *(Greece)*	122
Hummus Bowl *(Greece)*	124
Parsley Pesto *(Greece)*	120

India

Carrot Pesto *(India)*	152
Coconut Barfi *(India)*	156
Ramen Salad *(India)*	154

Iran

Naan Bread *(Iran)*	150
Onion Pesto *(Iran)*	146
Roast Beef Pinwheels *(Iran)*	148

Italy

Eggplant Parmesan Lasagna Stacks *(Italy)*	112
Risotto-Stuffed Peppers *(Italy)*	110
Zucchini Pesto *(Italy)*	108

Japan

Daikon Pesto *(Japan)*	176
Edamame *(Japan)*	180
Sushi Stack *(Japan)*	178

Korea

Celery Pesto *(Korea)*	170
Korean Egg Roll *(Korea)*	172
Millet Burgers *(Korea)*	174

Malaysia

Kuih Puffs *(Malaysia)*	184
Lemongrass Pesto *(Malaysia)*	182
Shrimp Satay *(Malaysia)*	186

Mayan

Mushroom and Chia Pesto *(Mayan)*	22
Salisbury Steak *(Mayan)*	26
Tamale Cups *(Mayan)*	24

(The) Midwest United States

Crispy Gnocchi *(Midwest United States)*	38
Kale Salad *(Midwest United States)*	36
Pecan Pesto (Midwest United States)	34

Morocco

Couscous Salad *(Morocco)*	204
Lamb with Candied Fruit *(Morocco)*	206
Spices Pesto *(Morocco)*	202

Mozambique

Cassava Pesto *(Mozambique)*	232
Tomato Cobbler *(Mozambique)*	234
Watermelon Ceviche *(Mozambique)*	236

Myanmar

Bamboo Shoots Salad *(Myanmar)*	196
Lemon Pesto *(Myanmar)*	194
Tapioca Pudding *(Myanmar)*	198

Native American

Cranberry Nausamp *(Native American)*	20
Pumpkin Pesto *(Native American)*	16
Stuffed Turkey Meatloaf *(Native American)*	18

New York

Chef Salad *(New York)*	44
Green Bean Pesto *(New York)*	40
Reuben Pizza *(New York)*	42

New Zealand
- Afghan Biscuits *(New Zealand)* — 252
- Breakfast Sausages *(New Zealand)* — 254
- Eggplant Pesto *(New Zealand)* — 250

Nigeria
- Peanut Stew *(Nigeria)* — 212
- Plantain Bread *(Nigeria)* — 210
- Yam Pesto *(Nigeria)* — 208

Peru
- Asparagus Pesto *(Peru)* — 58
- Quinoa Soup *(Peru)* — 60
- Street Corn *(Peru)* — 62

Puerto Rico
- Caribbean Coleslaw *(Puerto Rico)* — 54
- Passion Fruit Pesto *(Puerto Rico)* — 52
- Piña Colada *(Puerto Rico)* — 56

Russia
- Cherry Pesto *(Russia)* — 158
- Marshmallows *(Russia)* — 162
- Oatmeal Bars *(Russia)* — 160

South Africa
- Corn Pesto *(South Africa)* — 238
- Mealie Casserole *(South Africa)* — 242
- Sorghum Pilaf *(South Africa)* — 240

Southern United States
- Collard Greens Pesto *(Southern United States)* — 28
- Deviled Eggs *(Southern United States)* — 30
- Succotash *(Southern United States)* — 32

Spain
- Melon Gazpacho *(Spain)* — 80
- Red Cabbage Pesto *(Spain)* — 78
- Spanish Tortilla *(Spain)* — 82

Sweden
- Rutabaga Pesto *(Sweden)* — 96
- Swedish Tuna Balls *(Sweden)* — 100
- Sweet Buns *(Sweden)* — 98

Switzerland
- Barley Minestrone *(Switzerland)* — 106
- Leek Galette *(Switzerland)* — 104
- Swiss Chard Pesto *(Switzerland)* — 102

Thailand
- Mango Pesto *(Thailand)* — 188
- Red Pepper Salad *(Thailand)* — 190
- Yellow Chicken Curry *(Thailand)* — 192

Uganda
- Banana Pesto *(Uganda)* — 226
- Cassava Muffins *(Uganda)* — 230
- Spiced Chicken *(Uganda)* — 228